THE
BIRTHDAY
PARTY
BOOK

BY

JEREMY SAGE

☆

WITH

KATHRYN WATTERSON

▫

ILLUSTRATIONS BY

STEVEN GUARNACCIA

Clarkson N. Potter, Inc./Publishers
DISTRIBUTED BY
CROWN PUBLISHERS, INC.
NEW YORK

THE
BIRTHDAY
PARTY
BOOK

HOW TO GIVE YOUR CHILD A HAPPY BIRTHDAY

Publisher's Note: Many of the products and services that appear in this book are
trademarks of their respective companies. Every effort has been made to identify these
trademarks by initial capitalization. Should there be an omission in this respect, we shall
be pleased to make the necessary corrections in future printings.

Text copyright © 1987 by Jeremy Sage
Illustrations copyright © 1987 by Steven Guarnaccia

Published by Clarkson N. Potter, Inc., 225 Park Avenue South, New York,
New York, 10003 and represented in Canada by the Canadian MANDA Group
CLARKSON N. POTTER, POTTER, and colophon are trademarks of
Clarkson N. Potter, Inc.
Designed by Gael Towey • Manufactured in the United States of America

LIBRARY OF CONGRESS CATALOGING-IN-PUBLICATION DATA
Sage, Jeremy.
The birthday party book.

1. Children's parties.   2. Birthdays.
I. Watterson, Kathryn.   II. Title.
GV1205.S34   1987   793.2′1   86-22521
ISBN 0-517-56346-0

10 9 8 7 6 5 4 3 2 1
FIRST EDITION

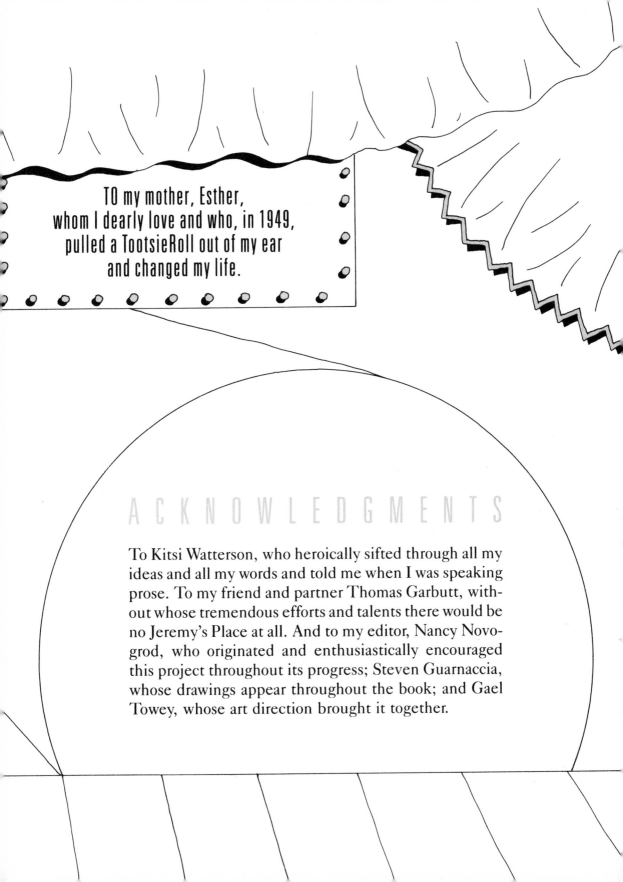

TO my mother, Esther,
whom I dearly love and who, in 1949,
pulled a TootsieRoll out of my ear
and changed my life.

ACKNOWLEDGMENTS

To Kitsi Watterson, who heroically sifted through all my ideas and all my words and told me when I was speaking prose. To my friend and partner Thomas Garbutt, without whose tremendous efforts and talents there would be no Jeremy's Place at all. And to my editor, Nancy Novogrod, who originated and enthusiastically encouraged this project throughout its progress; Steven Guarnaccia, whose drawings appear throughout the book; and Gael Towey, whose art direction brought it together.

or the past twenty-three years, I've been giving birthday parties for children. Two or three times a day, three hundred days a year, I greet, entertain, and celebrate the birthday child. My goal is always the same—to help children feel good.

If you ask any child who's come to one of my parties, "What's so special about Jeremy?" he'll probably say that Jeremy is "very funny." I do know what makes kids laugh. When I make peculiar monster faces, five- and six-year-olds laugh. When I chase Rubin the Robot or Rubin the Robot chases me, four- and five-year-olds laugh. When my fingers tap me on the shoulder and I look around to see who's interrupting me, only to discover that it's my own fingers, three-year-olds laugh. I know what kids like, but the truth of the matter is that they do, too. And so do you.

Birthday parties are meant to be fun! Almost any party will have some fun in it because children are naturally enthusiastic and they like just being together. The secret is figuring out how to keep them all

1

feeling that way for a whole party and, most important, how to make the birthday boy or girl feel special at the same time. If you know what to do and what to avoid, you can have a successful party that leaves everyone feeling good and gives the birthday child a wonderful memory.

I began working with children when I was a psychology major at Brandeis University and served as drama coach at two different Boston-area schools. During the summers, I was drama counselor at a number of children's camps.

The summer of 1968 was pivotal for me. I worked at a camp in upstate New York with Shelley Weiner, who, with his wife, Arleen, now owns and operates Camp Winadu in Massachusetts. Shelley was head counselor, and he was better with children than anyone I'd ever known. I'd never seen so many kids follow one person. He also had a concept that was new to me—he was running a "winter camp" in New York City, an after-school sports program called the All Stars.

In the fall I moved to New York, started graduate school in the theater program at Columbia University, and went to work for the All Stars. I drove a minivan and picked up the children after school, took them ice-skating or ball playing, and then dropped them off at home. I had the only nontumultuous All Stars van because I told jokes and stories to entertain my passengers.

Then one day a woman called me up and said, "My daughters, Beryl and Robin, love your stories. Do you think you could come over to our house for Beryl's birthday party? She's going to be seven, and she'd love for you to just do what you do on the bus!" I went, and, when it was over, Beryl's mom gave me a shirt—a nice shirt. It came from Saks Fifth Avenue and I thought it was just great.

A couple of days later, another parent called up and asked, "Are you the party entertainer?" I said, "Well, yes, I guess so." She said she'd like me to entertain at her son's birthday party, and she asked me how much I charged. I said, "The last mom gave me a shirt." She said, "Well, Jeremy, I'll give you some money and you can buy your own shirt." That was thousands of birthday parties ago.

The title I would have liked for this book—"Excuse Me, Is It Beluga?"—came from one particular party that took place early in my career. The birthday child was the five-year-old son of a diplomatic attaché in New York City, and the party was held in the grand, formal living room of the diplomat's Fifth Avenue town house. All the children were in dress attire. A waiter came around with a silver tray of caviar. Caviar! One of the five-year-olds took a cracker from the tray and then looked up at the waiter, who was wearing a white jacket, black pants, and a bow tie. His voice echoed into the vastness of the room when he asked the waiter, "Excuse me, is it Beluga?"

During this time, my theater career was also starting up. I began acting Off Broadway in plays, musicals, and improvisational comedy groups, but kept on giving birthday parties in the afternoons. In 1972, I got the role of Jesus in the road show of *Godspell*. We performed in over 250 cities in 42 states in 10 months. I then did six months of *Godspell* Off Broadway and was lucky enough to move with the show when it finally came to Broadway. I have the curious distinction of being the last Jesus on the Great White Way.

When the show closed in the fall of 1977, I made some TV commercials and voice-overs (that was me with Brooke Shields in the original ad for Calvin Klein jeans), and all the while I played the birthday-party circuit. One day I got a call for a big commercial, and I said, "I'm already booked." The agent asked, "With whom? We'll get it changed." I said, "This can't be changed. It's a birthday party and I never miss a show."

I realized that I had inadvertently made a very big decision. I wanted to do birthday parties more than I wanted to do commercials, and more than I wanted to act on someone else's stage. It also was clear that I wanted a theater of my own to give parties in. I called my friend Thomas Garbutt in Wisconsin, and said, "Please come here and start a birthday party business with me. You build the sets and scenery and we'll be partners." Chief, as Thomas is known to the kids, had made sets for the shows at Camp Winadu when he was creativity counselor there. I can't think of anyone who could have brought more imagination and talent to the job.

In 1982, I rented a small second-floor space on uptown Madison Avenue in New York City, and Chief started creating Jeremy's Place. I said, "I want it like theater." And that's just what it was. Chief is a magician at making places look wonderful and fanciful. Once I asked him to create a backdrop of New York City, and he made an entire skyline, with little blinking lights on it and an elevated track with electric trains. Chief can take ugly pipes and narrow passageways and turn them into trees and tunnels that convey a sense of excitement and adventure. In 1985, we moved to a larger place—Jeremy's Place II—where Chief continues to extend his web of enchantment.

At a typical Jeremy's Place party, I greet the children on the sidewalk and send them down the Magic Tunnel to the Party Room, where Chief shows them around, explains the rules, does the opening act, and makes it all work. He listens to everything the kids ask and takes the time to answer every question. He's stricter than I am—sort of the teacher everyone likes, while I'm the funny uncle.

We treat each birthday party just like theater. We have lighting for the stage, and we dim the lights for the audience. Every show we give has a beginning, a middle, and an end. There's the Overture, the Main Act, and the Closing Number, with dozens of prizes and jokes and happenings carefully tucked in between. Everything is timed precisely. Every activity is planned from the moment the children set foot inside Jeremy's Place until the party is over and they're outside again.

We believe that this is the birthday person's day, and we try our best to make it a day to be remembered. The birthday person's seat is special, and his or her end of the table is brighter. There is a pink spotlight over his or her head. And by the way, Beryl, the seven-year-old of my first party, is now twenty-four years old. She's the cameraperson who videotapes shows at Jeremy's Place.

You don't have to do exactly what we do to have a good birthday party. When you give a birthday party for your child, it doesn't have to be *Godspell* or Ringling Brothers. But the principles involved are the same. The party should be fun, and your child should be the star of the show. My hope is that this book will show you how to make it happen.

To all of you birthday parents and birthday children, I wish you parties that give you the most lively, loving, fun and the best times ever. Happy birthday!

Birthday parties celebrate the birthday person and welcome in his* new age. He receives presents and privileges in front of his friends. He's the center of attention and the acknowledged star of the day.

. . . .

Writing the Script

A birthday party should be exciting, fun, and joyful. It should have all the drama and thrill of good theater. The secrets of a good party are *planning* and *structure*. In this book, I intend to share those secrets.

Even a very simple birthday party should be carefully preplanned, organized, and rehearsed. Every minute of the event, from start to finish, should be accounted for in the script. Just as in the theater, you have to make decisions.

QUESTIONS TO ASK YOURSELF

Who's the star of the show? (It's the birthday person.)

Who are the supporting cast? (They are the guests.)

Who's the producer/director? (That's you.)

What are the show's beginning, middle, and end? What is the Opening Number? What's the Main Performance? How does the show close?

What about the staging? Who sits where?

Who's stage manager? Who will lower the lights when the birthday cake comes out? Who will hold the door open?

What props do you need? When it's time to light the candles, will there be a mad scramble for a lighter that works?

Write the script so that it builds excitement and expectations. Eliminate the unexpected. The surprises should look spontaneous, but they must be carefully choreographed. A theatrical atmosphere height-

---

* I give as many birthday parties for girls as boys, but from now on I'll say "he," "him," and "his," because the standard usage is simpler than constantly repeating "he or she," "him or her," and "his or hers."

ens ordinary experiences; it conveys the feeling that something extraordinary is happening and is going to happen. For a birthday party, let the children smell the greasepaint everywhere. Just as a true theater experience begins with the taking of tickets and leads through the climactic moments of drama to the finale, so too the best birthday party experience begins with the greetings at the door and builds to the drama of the cake ceremony and the singing of "Happy Birthday."

At a good birthday party, it's fun to see the curtain come up and watch the show unfold.

. . . .

Building the Drama

Any birthday party that actively engages everyone's attention and interest is good. It doesn't have to be elaborate. The theatrical flair is in the way you build anticipation—not in anything complicated or fancy. My Aunt Rivie taught me that. She taught me how to use drama for a celebration.

Aunt Rivie used to say, "Let's make a party!" and you knew something special was going to happen. You knew you were going to celebrate. Aunt Rivie would make a party for me and my cousins Judy and Larry. A party given by Aunt Rivie meant that we sat at a special table with a special tablecloth and ate blueberries and cottage cheese. Nothing could be simpler, but it was always a fantastic experience.

Aunt Rivie would spread a colorful tablecloth over the table and then bring out her matching cups and plates. There were three colors—red, blue, and green—and she let us choose which one we wanted. She made a big ceremony out of giving us our cups. "Here's the red cup for you!" she would say, "and here's the blue cup for you! And here's the green cup for you!" The way she said it, she gave us each the feeling we'd picked the *right* color. Then she'd serve us all a mound of cottage cheese with a little ring of blueberries around the bottom and one blueberry on top—not dumped off to the side, but right on top. That was special! That was a party! I loved it, and I love Aunt Rivie for teaching me the great fun and anticipation of a party.

8

Making the Child Feel Important

Parents need to remember this rule of thumb about a birthday: the birthday person is hypersensitive about everything, while the other children often could care less. For instance, some of the guests may find it funny to sing, "You look like a monkey and smell like one, too," but this can completely overshadow the rest of the party for the birthday child unless an adult steps in and stops the song. The remedy to any such unhappy situation is doing it again and doing it right. Tell the children, "We don't sing the song like that. Esther's birthday is a very special occasion. We only do this once a year, so let's try it again and do it right."

The birthday person is ready to be king or queen for the day, ready to be loved, ready for magic, ready for the red-carpet treatment. A child who wants so much to be the center of attention is particularly vulnerable. If he does not get treated in a special way and is not attended to, he will feel as if he's been kicked in the shins. Certainly, rudeness, indifference, or even simple lack of attention can be devastating. It destroys the day, and, hence, the memory.

Respect for the child makes a successful party. Respect for the child is *key* to making your child happy at his birthday party. It's key to his remembering the day with pleasure.

9

. . . .

The Guest List

Deciding whom to invite is the first block to building a good party—and it's one on which the entire construction can rise or fall.

Consider the age of your child and his friends. This will help you tap your common sense; obviously, ten eight-year-olds will be easier to handle than ten two-year-olds. Remember: For the birthday person to have a memorable day, you need to have a manageable group.

Consult your child. He may have very specific ideas about whom he wants, whom he doesn't want, and why, and his wishes will probably be appropriate to his age. If he's four or five, for instance, he may want boys *and* girls, and won't care if the guests are from different schools and don't know one another. If he's seven, more likely he'll want only the *boys* who are in his class. A nine-year-old rarely wants children who are outside his closest group. He won't want cousins or acquaintances who will "ruin" his party. If these choices seem reasonable and don't cause a major political problem or crisis of conscience, you should honor them. Make your child feel good about his decisions.

From my experiences with parties, I have my own preferences about numbers of guests. I think there should be at least ten to twelve children to create a real atmosphere of festivity at a party for a child who is five or older. Although some people believe you should have the same number of guests as the age of the child (four guests for a four-year-old's party, and so on), I think a group that small is a gathering—not a party. However, in the interest of maintaining control, I recommend no more than eighteen children at any party. This figure isn't set in stone, but it seems to work the best.

I have no concern about whether the guests are all girls, all boys, or both sexes. That's up to the birthday person, but I think the mix of ages is important because a party depends on the combined activity of a number of people. The pleasure of *all* the guests determines the party's success. The reason I try not to mix three-, five-, and eight-year-olds, for instance, is the same reason educators don't put children these ages together in the classroom. Pleasure, like learning, depends to a large extent on homogeneous, age-appropriate activities.

Here are some points I've learned about age and birthday parties:

One-Year-Olds. Children this age are not going to anticipate or remember a birthday party. If you want to celebrate your one-year-old's birthday with a party, just remember that the party is more for you than for your child. Be careful not to overwhelm or frighten him.

Don't invite more than four or five babies and their parents. Try to have babies who are roughly the same age—eighteen months and under; older children will be bored by the immaturity of the younger guests. The babies' parents must be with them at all times, and, essentially, it is a party for them. Make it as quiet and as easy on the parents and the babies as possible.

Two-Year-Olds. Any party is as good as its weakest link—and with two-year-olds, there are bound to be plenty of weak links. No entertainment works for a group of two-year-olds, and no structure. Don't expect group activity. Don't expect focus or sustained attention. These children can have fun around the table together but not much more than that. Invite three to eight children with adults who will stay for the entire party. Parents or baby-sitters must be with their two-year-olds at all times because each guest needs a supervisor. Don't invite older children to a two-year-old's party unless you want to watch power struggles. The best thing to do for a two-year-old's party is to wait until he's three.

Three-Year-Olds. Three-year-olds are at the beginning stages of real socializing. They can suspend the *me, me, me*'s for short periods of time and form a cohesive group for a party. You can say to three-year-olds, "We're all going to sit in a circle"—and it can happen. Three-year-olds can enjoy one another's company, can share a little bit and be entertained. You can capture their attention for short periods of time, and get them to laugh and feel part of the group.

Don't invite more than eight to twelve children. Threes are a year unto themselves: You cannot invite two-year-olds and expect them to mingle. You can invite a four-year-old, if you think that child will be

11

supportive of the birthday person. Most three-year-olds are not ready to be left alone at a party; each guest this age should have an adult with him. Although parents may not need to stay in the same room, they should still be nearby, within sight or at least sound of their child. We call this the "invisible umbilical." Also be alert to the differences among your three-year-old invitees. Three years and three months is a lot different from three years and nine months in terms of independence and sociability, while two years and eight months usually means two.

Four-Year-Olds. At the age of four, children enter the birthday-party circuit. They begin anticipating their own birthday party months before the event. Four-year-olds have a much longer sharing time than younger children. They have more self-control and have learned how to function in groups.

Invite ten to fifteen children. Inviting a three-year-old guest is not a good idea unless the child is close to his fourth birthday. Best for this age is all four-year-olds, and perhaps one or two five-year-olds who can join the fun. Parents can drop off their children and pick them up at the end of the party unless a child seems uncomfortable with this arrangement. A four-year-old who marches right in will probably be fine left alone. One who digs his fingernails into the doorjamb to avoid entry is suspect.

Five-Year-Olds. Invite from twelve to fifteen five-year-olds. A sociable four-year-old can also be included and will probably make the birthday child feel grown-up. Five-year-olds for the most part are independent and don't need their parents to stay

 DO'S AND DON'TS

When you're looking at a party room:

Do make sure the furniture is movable so you can set the room up the way *you* want it to be. Bolted-down furniture leaves you stuck with a single floor plan. If the management says you cannot move the furniture, choose another room.

Do find a room that has a private bathroom attached to it. You don't want other customers walking through the birthday room to go to the bathroom. This will disrupt the party. If you like the room but it doesn't have a private bathroom, decide whether you can have an adult on duty to walk children to and from the public bathroom.

Do find a one-level room that doesn't have steps, ledges, or orchestra pits to swallow children. Make sure it is not so large that guests will wander off and get lost.

Do find a room that has carpet on the floor, not concrete.

Do find a light room. Kids, like plants, are positively phototropic. Accept a dark room only if there are extra lamps that will accommodate 100-watt light bulbs you can bring along to replace the regular lights.

Do find a room where you can bring your own birthday cake—unless the restaurant makes one to your liking.

Do remember to ask if there's a freezer for your ice cream or ice-cream cake. (If they don't have a freezer you can use, do you have a cooler to keep the ice cream frozen?)

Do think about the atmosphere. Do you have to walk through a singles bar to get to the party room? That is *not* a nice atmosphere for children. For single fathers and mothers, maybe, yes, but not for kids.

. . . .

**Places
with
Built-in
Entertainment**
. . . .

Your child might like having his birthday party at a place that features activities or entertainment he particularly enjoys—for instance, a skating rink, zoo, or puppet theater. I personally prefer the flexibility of a room at home or in a restaurant where it is easiest to ensure that the birthday person is the star of the day. However, parties at public spots can be successful, too, as long as the guests share the birthday child's enthusiasm for the activities or entertainment.

When you're taking a group of children six and younger to a public place, make certain that you pin a tag on each child with his name and *your* phone number (older children might find this embarrassing). Have someone stay at home by your phone. Tell the kids before you leave the house, or at the entrance to the place, that you will show them a centrally located spot where they should go if they get lost. Be sure that you have everyone's attention when you point out the spot. Then just stay alert so that no one goes astray.

If you think your child would like having a party at a place with built-in entertainment, go to see it first. Watch a show or part of one. Join a tour or peek in on a party that's in session and observe. Are the kids having a good time? Don't pick a place that makes extra work for you. There will be enough to do managing the dynamics of the party.

QUESTIONS TO ASK YOURSELF

Can we serve cake and ice cream here? Is there a room or an area where the group can be gathered together after the event?

What are your responsibilities—for example, must you supply the paper plates, juice, and cups?

Is there a refrigerator or a spot where you can safely leave the cooler and boxes until you're ready for them?

Can you set up a table the way you want it or lay a tarpaulin on the floor?

Can the group sing "Happy Birthday"?

If the answer to any of these questions is no and you still want to have the party there, consider whether you're close enough to go home (or somewhere else appropriate—an informal restaurant or pizza parlor, for example) for the meal or the cake and candle-lighting ceremony. You might have the food beforehand and then go to the party place. Check out where you will have the food as carefully as you do everything else. You *must* have cake and ice cream, and you *must* be allowed to sing "Happy Birthday." Nothing imperative should be left to chance or the last minute.

Some popular public places for parties include:

Behind-the-Scenes Places. These can be bakeries, post offices, soda bottling plants, newspaper printing plants, bookbinding shops, or bagel, pretzel, or potato chip factories. What's great about conveyor-belt places is that the process is the central entertainment and it teaches the kids something interesting. Again, getting there can be part of the show.

Children's Theaters. A play, holiday presentation, storyteller, or puppet show may interest the birthday child and his guests. Inquire whether there's a room at  the theater for a private birthday party following the performance. Perhaps the stage can be used. Make sure that yours will be the only party in the space, or the setting will be too chaotic and will dilute the focus and the magic of the celebration.

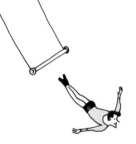

Circuses. The circus is always exciting for children, but these parties work best with smaller groups. You'll be more likely to maintain group cohesion and keep track of six rather than twenty guests. Find out from the circus staff if there's something special the children can do before the show starts or at intermission. Could they be in the opening parade? See the elephants up close? Meet the people on the flying trapeze?

Gyms. If the gym is small and your child is good at gymnastics, he may enjoy a gym party. Unless the gym offers a party program, though, the event can simply be too ordinary— too everyday. Unorganized gym parties are like traveling from point A to point B in a green Chevy. A real party is like traveling in a stretch limousine. Both vehicles get you there, but which trip is memorable? Find out ahead of time if instructors can give an active forty-five-minute class for the children and there is a party area for after the class.

Ice-Skating Rinks. If your child loves ice-skating or roller-skating, and he and his friends are all able to skate, a rink can be a good spot for a party. Unless the rink is very small, however, or a section can be reserved for your group alone, it's not a setting where the birthday person can get a lot of attention. Skating parties are also twice as much work for the parents and have some inherent dangers: Kids can get hurt or get lost in the crowd.

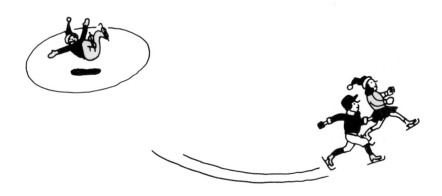

Movies. If the movie is one that your child is enthusiastic about seeing and you feel is appropriate to his age group, a movie party can provide good entertainment without too much work and worry for parents. However, the guests must be seven or older to maintain proper movie theater decorum (no talking, yelling, squirming, or spitball throwing). Think of ways you can make the outing special—and give the birthday person a chance to be the center of attention. (See page 30 for ideas on getting to the party.)

Museums. Some children's museums and traditional art museums have birthday party programs. They may provide tours, arts and crafts projects, audience-participation plays, or talks on subjects of interest to elementary school children. Ask what the museum offers, and whether there's a place to serve cake and ice cream.

Parks or Nature Reserves. If your child loves the outdoors, the weather is warm, and you can set an alternative rain date, consider having a party for children of five and up at a park or environmental center. Many parks have rangers or tour guides on their staff who will show children where the underground animals live; how to find frogs, ladybugs, woodpeckers, and robins; how to identify trees by their leaves and bark; and how to plant bulbs or prune bushes. Members of the park staff may even supervise them on work projects that last up to an hour and a half. Remember to bring the bug repellent.

Swimming Pools. Swim parties are fun *only* if all the children enjoy swimming. These parties are most difficult with a group five and younger because two or three children are always afraid of the water. Why have a party where *anybody* is afraid?

Zoos. It's always fun to take kids to the zoo, and there's usually an area—a party room or a covered outdoor space— where you can arrange to have the meal or cake and ice cream. Find out whether the zoo offers special programs. Will staff members tell the children about the animals? Consider the age and personalities of the children who will be at the party. The zoo is a large place. Is this group polite and demure or wild and unmanageable? Do *they* belong in the zoo? If the children are at least six years old and can cooperate with a tightly controlled schedule, the zoo can be a fabulous place for a party.

DISASTERS TO AVOID

When you have the party outside your home, remember that you do not have complete control. For instance, it's not unimaginable that when you show up at the restaurant, the children's room at the museum, or the gym, you might find another party going on in *your* space! The afternoon or night manager may have booked another party for the same time, not noticing what the day manager noted (or didn't note) on another part of the page.

You can avoid this kind of terrible mixup if you make three confirming telephone calls—two weeks before the party, a week before the party, and the day before the party. Take a different, and friendly, approach with each call. Confirm the time, date, and number of guests, the number of chairs that are available, or any other detail that justifies the call.

If you're too embarrassed to make repeated calls, ask a friend to fill in: "We lost my son's invitation to a birthday party. Is this the place where the party for Ronnie Jones is taking place on May 30?''

Most errors can be avoided. For this party, they *must* be avoided.

c h a p t e r

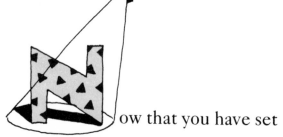

ow that you have set
the stage, how do you decide on the content of the script?
What are you going to do for your Overture? What should
you have for the Main Show?

If the party is to be held at home or in a restaurant,
the entertainment should be carefully planned. Here's
where you get to make and keep the children happy—and
show your stuff as a producer and director of the event.

If you're having the party outside the home, the Overture can be
going to the destination. A festive trip will enhance the excitement of
the Main Event. Could you hire a horse-drawn wagon, a little school

bus, or even a limousine? What about decorating your station wagon? Take a special route—through a tunnel, underneath a bridge, or by Grandma's house for a prearranged cookie break.

You need to know all about the production before you buy your party goods or make out the invitations, just in case special purchases are required or directions are needed to the party place.

The Grand Entrance

One way to announce the glamour of the event—and make your guests feel important—is to have a person with a home video camera tape the children as they arrive at the party. This turns all the guests into instant celebrities, and gives you and your child a souvenir. As a major bonus, the tape can be played back as the closing activity, and the children will be able to see themselves on television— which they love, no matter what age they are.

If you don't own a video camera, you can rent one quite inexpensively, along with a video cassette recorder (VCR), which can be hooked up to your television. Have a responsible person do the taping for the party, and be sure the birthday child makes a cameo appearance at the start; the birthday sister and brother should be introduced as well. Your cameraperson should get closeups of the guests one by one as they enter, and of the birthday child greeting them.

The Overture

The first warm-up activity should begin once the children seem comfortable with one another and adjusted to the place—approximately fifteen to twenty minutes after the first guests arrive. (More about pace and timing in Chapter 8.)

There are a number of short projects that make excellent overtures for a children's party.

Building Cities, Castles, or Walls. Even though wooden blocks are common at nursery school and in kindergarten and first-grade classrooms, young children never seem to tire of working with them. You can put small groups of children ages three to five to work on joint projects, such as building a castle or a block city. Parents and helpers can assist.

Decorating T-Shirts. Buy simple white T-shirts (boys' undershirts will do), fabric markers, glue-on glitter, fabric peel-off and press-on decorations, or fat stickers called ''puffies and oilies'' that adhere to material (available at five-and-tens or fabric stores). If you want to be fancy, dye the bottom half of each T-shirt in your bathtub or washing machine. Set up a large table at the party with the markers and other material. Children aged seven through eleven will like decorating the shirts in any way they please, and creating their own favors to take home after the party.

Drawing on Butcher Paper. Tape some of this inexpensive brown paper around the walls, and, using a one-half-inch-wide Magic Marker, divide the paper into large rectangles. To avoid damaging the walls and your guests' clothing, use water-soluble markers, and never use black or brown ones—they're dreary. Put the children's names at the top of the spaces so they'll know where to go to make their murals, and lay out markers or crayons on a nearby table. Once the drawings are completed (about fifteen minutes), the helpers should cut out each child's work for him to take home at the end of the party. Children ages four through six will particularly enjoy this activity.

Making Crowns. Cut strips of white or colored construction paper and lay them out around a table with colored markers and/or bowls of sequins and glitter, and four or five glue sticks. The crowns can be stapled together to wear during the party and taken home afterward. (Make sure you *don't* make a cone-shaped 'dunce cap.' Even out of lightweight paper, those points can hurt one's eye.) Four-, five-, and six-year-olds will enjoy this project and so will nursery-schoolers with some help.

Making Place Mats. Supply each child with light-colored construction paper cutouts (ovals, squares, butterflies—a variety of imaginative shapes will do). The place mats can be blank or can contain the outline of a car, house, tree, or rainbow to be colored in. Lay out a supply of washable crayons or markers in pastel shades. Provide stickers for embellishment. Children aged four through seven will enjoy this.

Posing for Portraits. If you're not making a video, a fun warm-up activity for children of all ages is having instant portraits taken. If, and only if, the birthday person is agreeable to it, you can pose him with each guest. Kids love watching their images come into focus as the picture develops. For funny-face instant portraits, cut a hole in the center of a plain white plastic window shade (available at variety stores), and draw a funny face on each side around the opening. For instance, draw cat ears and whiskers on one side and a gorilla face on the other. Ask each child, "Do you want to be a gorilla or a cat?" Have your helper hold up the shade and let the child stand behind it and put his face through the hole. Joke stores carry silly eyeglasses with a nose attached—a great prop, too.

. . . .

Party Games and Prizes

arty games can also serve as opening activities—on their own or after a project. Although I tend to avoid them because of their potential for over-competitiveness and hurt feelings, well-chosen and well-run games are good time fillers that help to focus the group's attention.

A good game should be fun. It should involve the whole group—unlike Pin the Tail on the Donkey, where only one child is involved at any one time and all the others must wait. (Picture being the nineteenth child in line!) Usually, one formal game per party is enough. In an informal way, I like to make games out of almost everything to keep the children on their toes. "Who knows what color this is? Who can guess how many plates we have here?"

Games also give you an opportunity to hand out prizes—one prize to the winner, one prize to the child who comes in second or even third, and one prize to the birthday person because he's the birthday person! Before a game starts, I often ask, "How many people want to have a chance to win a prize? Everybody? Okay, well only one person will win the prize, but everybody gets to play, and that's fun, isn't it?"

If you decide to have a formal game at your birthday party, choose one that contains some drama, adventure, challenge, or reward. It should pass the Green Penny Hunt test—a standard based on a game you'll see below that is always a success. Will it make the kids feel good? Will it be fun and an adventure for each child? Here are some of my suggestions for games:

Add-to games. The old "I went to the store and bought . . ." always produces a lot of giggles. Have the children sit in a circle and instruct them to remember what was said before. With six- through eight-year-olds, it's easiest to go in alphabetical order: "I went to the store and bought an apple, . . . bread, . . . crackers, . . . a dog, . . . an elephant, . . . a flying fish, . . . a gorilla, . . . a horrible horse . . ." With older children, random additions can get pretty funny and ridiculous. Twice around the circle is usually more than enough. Everyone's a winner.

Bingo. Bingo is a fun party game for eight-year-olds and up because it's fast, can be done in a group, and involves lots of prizes. Try to rent or borrow an electric Bingo set that lights up and beeps out numbers, and remember to call out the numbers enthusiastically.

Duck, Duck, Goose. Sit the children in a circle and have the birthday child walk around the outside, lightly tapping each child on the head with his hand or, even better, a silly rubber squeaker hammer. The birthday child says "Duck" as he taps each guest, until he comes to a particular child he decides to declare "Goose." The birthday child then scurries around the circle again in the same direction, while the goose springs to his feet and tries to tag him (gently, please) before the birthday child sits down in the goose's spot. If the birthday child reaches the place untagged, the game continues with the former goose as the stroller. If the birthday child is tagged, the goose returns to his spot and the birthday child must stroll around tapping heads again. This is a great game that will keep eight to fifteen four- and five-year-olds amused for around ten minutes.

The Green Penny Hunt. A few days before the party, lay out 250 pennies on waxed paper and spray-paint them neon green. Hide them before the guests arrive. Each green penny is worth one point, and the children with the most points win first, second, and third prizes. Of course, it's finders keepers for the pennies. This game is best played outdoors.

Guessing Game. This is a game to play with five- to eight-year-olds at the party table. Place a large glass bottle decorated with ribbon, stickers, or paint and filled with between fifty and eighty-five jelly beans in the center of the table. Tell the children, "Between fifty and eighty-five jelly beans are in the bottle. I want you to guess how many there are. I'll come around and write down the number you choose." After everyone's number is written down, pour the jelly beans out of the bottle and count them one by one. Pass out the first thirty or so jelly beans (twice around the table) to all the children as you are counting. Put the rest back in the bottle while continuing the count. Whoever has guessed the right number, or closest to it, without going over it, wins the bottle and its contents.

Mad-Libs. Children eight years old and over will love the short stories they create themselves by filling in these pads. A parent or helper can be in charge of providing clues to the missing words ("Name a disgusting insect," "Name an icky food," "Name one of your teachers"). An adult then dramatically reads the story back. Mad-Libs pads are available at stationery and toy stores.

Ping-Pong and Pinball. If you're having a party for children eight and older, they can play round-robin pinball or Ping-Pong in the basement or playroom until they hear your prearranged signal. At the sound of a horn, for instance, they'll know they have five minutes to get upstairs for the main entertainment.

DISASTERS TO AVOID

When in doubt, I would always choose *not* to have a costume party. It's great to plan a costume party, but it's not nearly as much fun to have one. That's because the many difficulties in wearing costumes detract from the fun.

Most costumes involve plastic of some sort, and they become hot and uncomfortable. Angel wings get in the way when children are trying to eat; hats break; moustaches itch. Even worse, children can become upset that they're not wearing what the other guests are wearing. If they wear their Halloween costumes to a birthday party that falls before the holiday, there are bound to be incidents where costumes get stained, torn, or broken. Unfortunately, Snow White is usually a sloppy eater. Just anticipating not being able to wear a costume for Halloween often turns laughter into tears. If the party person has his heart set on costumes, let the children make an entrance in their costumes and have a costume parade—perhaps on video; then the children should take their costumes off and put them aside for the rest of the party.

. . . .

The Main Act

he main entertainment at a birthday party is like the Main Act of a Broadway show. It makes the strongest impression. It's the price of the ticket.

For parties at home when playing outdoors is not an option, or parties at restaurants, I strongly recommend hiring a professional entertainer for the Main Act. These people are trained to get and hold attention in a way that Daddy reading a story, Uncle Alfred doing his Donald Duck impersonations, or Big Sister and Brother putting on a puppet show cannot. You need someone who can occupy at least a half hour of party time in order to keep the group happy and avoid mayhem. Children tend to become restless when indoors. Trying to stretch out projects and games won't help. The party pace calls for a variety of activities, building to the high point that a performer will create.

If you feel a strong resistance to hiring an entertainer or are unable to find one in your area, there is an alternative I can recommend. A good short children's video film will often work if it's properly presented. Make "movie tickets" and hand them out; create a "theater" area and have "ushers" (helpers) show the guests to their seats; pass out freshly made popcorn in large paper cups. The movie itself should not last longer than fifteen to twenty-five minutes or attention will wander, but the ceremony will help fill up the remaining Main Act time.

Keep your child in mind when you're looking for an entertainer. What does the birthday person enjoy? Magic? Mime? Puppets? Art? Songs? Animals? Origami?

No matter where you live, though, if your child is a toddler, don't bother looking into entertainment. Although quiet entertainers such as folk singers can sometimes work for two-year-olds, they're entirely extraneous. Most toddlers would rather eat, explore one another's toys and bang a spoon on the table or on a fellow guest than pay attention to a performer for more than three minutes.

Ask around. What have people in your region been doing? Is there someone they've been using for parties who's a hit? Get references. If you've located the entertainer through the Yellow Pages or through an ad in a magazine, make doubly sure you get references—*recent* references. Never hire someone exclusively on what he says about himself. And never hire someone over the phone. If the entertainer is appearing somewhere, ask, "Can I peek in at the next party?" If he's entertaining in a shopping mall, ask him, "When can I look in to see some of your show?" A good entertainer should not take offense at your request. A good one who does take offense is not worth working with, because his attitude is wrong.

If the entertainer has the time, you should try to meet with him and discuss your child's likes and dislikes. It's usually a good idea for the birthday person to come along. If they hit it off, the birthday child will have a step up on his guests because he's a pal of the featured act. Also, meeting the birthday person will help the entertainer make the best plans possible for your child and his friends. Most entertainers have different presentations for different age groups. To make three-year-olds laugh, all they have to do is let a banana peel slide off their head, while with six-year-olds, monster faces create hilarity. By the way, if your child doesn't like or approve of the entertainer, choose someone else. Your child won't have a good time unless he enjoys the entertainment.

Let the entertainer know that he will be performing for no more than thirty to forty-five minutes—no longer than that. If he says he entertains for an hour and a half, tell him that his show will have to be shorter. This is a birthday party, not *Nicholas Nickleby*.

Remember, too, that it's not how much money you spend and how elaborate the routine that determine the success of the entertainment. Remember all those classic Broadway fiascos? They could have had thirty dancing gorillas and a big waterfall, but if the show wasn't any good, the event was a flop. You don't have to drop a skydiver on the tennis court to create a good party.

Simple acts can be wonderful.

Artists. If they bring along materials and teach the children to make something, artists can be really fun entertainers. The kids will have the satisfaction of participating as well as watching—and they'll have something to show for it when they're done. Origami experts are especially good for parties; your local children's museum may be able to supply a reference.

Balloon Sculptors. Children ages three to seven will enjoy watching animals being formed from long balloons and getting a poodle, dachsund, or other balloon creature to keep.

Clowns. Except for entertainers who do other things but use some clownlike makeup, they should generally be avoided. Most clowns are too scary for younger kids (especially one- through three-year-olds) and too silly for older ones. A clown is designed to entertain from a distance of forty feet or more. He's supposed to be larger than life. If you present him in real life, up close, he's too large. If you insist on having a clown, make sure he puts on his makeup as the children watch. At the least, this may dilute their fear of him. But don't count on it. The leap from reality to fantasy only takes a few seconds, and it's easy to forget that this huge being looked like a regular person a moment ago.

Comedians. Comedy for children is not the same as comedy for adults. When Don Rickles makes fun of somebody, it's very funny, but when a joke happens at the expense of a child's feelings, it's not. Even though children's comedy is what I do, I'm wary of comedians because I've seen too many bad examples of the genre.

Dog Acts. If a performing dog and the person on the other end of the leash are equally talented, the act can be lots of fun. The dog trainer might also give party guests tips on how to teach a simple trick to their own dogs.

Face Painters. They're all right for some nursery-school children, but there is bound to be a child or two who will not want his face painted, and some parents who worry about spoiling party clothes. If you are having a face painter, save the instant picture taking for part of the Main Event, instead of making it part of the Overture as described at the beginning of this chapter. Don't forget to keep one good shot for yourself!

Jugglers. Just make sure the one you hire is expert, or accidents can occur. A juggler who can teach a simple juggling act effectively may be a real hit, particularly with boys of seven, eight, and older.

Magicians. They can enthrall five- and six-year-olds. Seven-year-olds in particular like people to try to fool them! Sometimes you can arrange with the magician to teach the audience a simple trick to perform at home.

Storytellers. To work as the main event, they have to be stellar. A story is fine entertainment at school when weighed against lessons in addition and subtraction, but at a birthday party for lots of kids, something more Las Vegas is usually in order.

Sometimes unconventional entertainment can be a great hit. Use your imagination. How about hiring the man who drives the ice cream truck? Arrange with his company ahead of time to have him bring his truck by for a half hour to talk to the children about his work and pass out ice cream. Or, how about a volunteer fireman? Have him tell the group about fighting fires and lead a tour of the fire truck.

As long as the weather is on your side, your child's party can be an adventure. Good weather-contingent entertainment includes hayrides, carriage and horse-drawn buggy rides, and boat and ferry trips; or for children seven and up, an elevator ride to a beautiful rooftop view from the tallest building in town. The great outdoors can also remove some of the need for diversions and structure that parties must have when they take place within four walls. Party games (don't forget the Green Penny Hunt), catch, Frisbee, softball, or free play can keep the children occupied if they take place outdoors.

Whatever you choose for the entertainment, remember the importance of presentation. Lead up to it with some drama and flair. In theater, the unexpected is often the most memorable part. The entertainment for the party should have a quality of the unexpected—whether it's merely fun that produces unexpected laughter, the excitement of learning or doing something new, or the chance to win a prize.

PARTY FOOD

side from the birthday cake, which is of supreme importance, what food do you want to serve at the party? Should you serve hamburgers or just snacks of apple juice, potato chips, and carrot strips? How about pizza and soda? Some choices are better than others. A sandwich in the hand, for instance, is better than lasagna on the dress. The age of the guests, their energy level, and the time of day the party is given should determine your menu. However, let me assure you that food is the least consequential of all your decisions.

The menu you choose has very little, if any, relevance to the party's overall success. In fact, *you do not even have to serve a meal.* If the party is not during a mealtime—if it's, say, from 2:00 P.M. to 3:30 P.M.—there's no reason to serve anything other than cake, ice cream, and juice.

The exception to that rule is a party for two-year-olds. Eating is all to these creatures, and passing out food and drinks one by one at the table will be the primary entertainment. If you gather two-year-olds together for an hour, you'll need to provide lots of sandwiches, cookies, juice, and fruit in addition to the ice cream and cake.

For children of other ages, the excitement is in the party itself. Their appetites are for the activity around them, not for the food on their plates.

. . . .

For Lunch or Dinner

Whatever you serve, keep it simple. Go easy on yourself. Think about children's appetites, and offer child-size portions. One grandmother taught me to cut each precut piece of pizza in half the long way for young children. This makes it easier for the child to handle—and it's a size to fit the appetite. If you're serving hamburgers, cut the hamburgers in half. You're not doing anyone a favor by serving them too much food. If they want

SPILLED MILK

second helpings, they can have second helpings, but most of them will be too excited to eat that much.

KETCHUP &
MELTED ICE CREAM

Consider the color of the food and its "smearability." If it smears, don't serve it. The milk chocolate does melt in your mouth; the candy coating, however, melts in their hands and on your upholstery. Do you want candy coating all over your furniture? Crumbs are easier to deal with—but even then, make sure they match the rug.

You do not have to worry about being perfectly balanced, wholesome, nutritious, or haute cuisine. Most children prefer *pizza, hamburgers, hot dogs, and potato chips.* Keep in mind when planning,

HAMBURGER
WITH
M&M GARNISH

however, that hamburgers and hot dogs do lend themselves to the possibility of minor mishaps—mainly because mustard and ketchup containers rarely distinguish between plates and party clothes. Even if you pour the ketchup for young children, they usually manage to get it on their own arms or those of your chairs.

After a lot of experiments, I'm personally convinced that plain pizza—no anchovies, sausages, or pepperoni, thank you—is the best food to serve at a children's party. That's because most kids love it. What's more, they eat it. There are other advantages, too. You don't have any preparation, fuss, or muss. You can pick it up or have it

ICE CREAM
&
PIZZA

delivered right before the party, and wrap the box in towels to keep it warm. All you have to do at mealtime is cut it and serve. Even room-temperature pizza tastes good, and it won't burn anyone's tongue.

BOWL OF CANDY
& MILK

A combination of tuna fish sandwiches, carrot sticks, celery sticks, and potato chips also works well. Cut off the crusts: Sandwiches without crusts are special party food.

To be really fancy, get two cookie cutters and cut out the sandwiches. Instead of asking the guests if they want a sandwich, ask them if they want a dragon or a cow. If you don't want to give them their choice of shapes, give them their   choice of tuna fish or peanut butter and jelly.

CELESTIAL
SANDWICHES

Children love choices, but keep the choices simple. A choice of shape or content, not both. ("Both" goes something like this: "I want a peanut butter dragon, not a tuna fish monster! Oh, no! I wanted a tuna fish dragon! This is a peanut butter dragon!")

9 HOT DOG BANANA SPLIT WITH FRIES & HOT FUDGE

What do you do if one of the kids says, "I hate pizza!" or "I hate tuna fish!" The answer is simple: "You don't have to eat it. Just leave room for the cake and ice cream." Don't worry about it. If he doesn't want to eat, don't make an issue of it. He's not going to starve. Give him extra potato chips to tide him over. Parties are for fun, not for lessons in nutrition.

TUNA FISH ON BED OF POTATO CHIPS; BREAD ON THE SIDE

The same goes for drinks—give a choice of two: the drink of the day or water. If a child doesn't want apple juice, orange juice, milk, or water either, that's okay too. He's not going to suffer from dehydration at the party.

APPLE JUICE FLOAT

47

DISASTERS TO AVOID

Raisins or peanuts should not be served to two- or three-year-olds because there's always one who sticks small objects up his nose.

Grape juice should not be served unless you like the idea of permanent purple on your clothes or your couch.

Small children should not be allowed to pick their own plates off a tray. Everyone else's food may end up on the floor or on a lap.

Cups should not be filled with juice before the children sit down or they'll certainly get spilled when chairs are pulled in. Wait until the group is seated, and fill cups one by one after you have served the sandwiches or pizza. *Never fill them to the top.*

Standing on chairs at the table should not be permitted. You do not need to have children falling into the food or onto the floor.

. . . .

Food for the Adults

If you don't want parents to stay for the party, don't have food for them. However, if the party is for small children, you'll want their parents to be present, so you should plan something for them to eat. Serve finger foods that require napkins rather than plates: two or three kinds of cheeses, some crackers, and a bowl of seedless grapes; cut vegetables and a dip; or chips, a dip, and a bowl of olives or cherry tomatoes.

Set out glasses, cups, and beverages. Let the parents serve themselves. Don't have only wine. Always have a nonalcoholic option like club soda, soda, or juice as well.

If the party is for one-, two-, or three-year-olds, the adult food should be in the same room as the children's food—or at least within the sight-line of the kids—the "invisible umbilical." If the party is for four- and five-year-olds and some parents will be staying, they should be in an adjoining room with the door open. It's fine to have parents peeking in on the party, but they shouldn't be fully present unless they are working as helpers.

If the party is for six-, seven-, eight-, or nine-year olds and the parents will be staying, put the food for the grown-ups in a far-away room. Move the parents out. Kids this age need to feel autonomous, at least in front of their friends. They don't want their parents involved or observing.

. . . .

The Cake

The ceremony surrounding the cake is the climactic moment of the celebration, so the cake you decide to buy or bake should look very pretty and taste delicious. Whether it's plain, fancy, or fanciful, the birthday cake is the pièce de résistance of the party.

THE BLOB

THE LEANING
TOWER

THE
BALLERINA

THE CHECKERBOARD

THE SURFER

THE PIZZA PIE

THE CASTLE

THE CUPCAKE

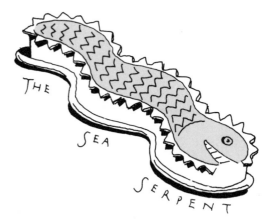

THE
SEA
SERPENT

I recommend ice-cream cake for birthday parties whenever it's possible. An ice-cream cake is easy to serve. It looks like a cake and has cake in it, but it's mostly ice cream—which, I find, children prefer. Another advantage is that the cake can be purchased weeks in advance and kept in the freezer.

If you're going to serve a real cake instead of an ice-cream cake, make sure you have ice cream or sherbet to go with it. Your chocolate cake or white cake may be delicious, but it needs ice cream for it to be truly festive and acceptable to children.

You can make suggestions, but let your child choose the kind of cake he wants, the kind of frosting, and the colors of the frosting, candles, and decorations. When you ask the questions, be open to the answers. If the birthday person wants green frosting, then he should have green frosting. Just add green food coloring to your shopping list.

Unless you're under specific instructions, try to make the cake as colorful as possible. Be sure, too, that there's either a single decoration for the birthday person or enough decorations for every child at the party. A cake with one flower is okay. A cake with twenty flowers is okay. A cake with three flowers is verboten. If there aren't enough for all the children, then there's a danger of tears and real disappointment.

An easy way to add color and keep everyone happy is to ring the top and the bottom of a home-baked or store-bought cake with M&M's candies. Every slice you serve will have candies on it. Unwrapped chocolate kisses can also be placed around the top of the cake, so that each child will get one.

DO'S AND DON'TS

Some things to keep in mind about the cake:

Don't wait until the last minute to bake or buy it. Make your plans well in advance of the party. If you're serving an ice-cream cake, order it, pick it up, and put it in your freezer as soon as you can. Have all the accessories for the cake, including the birthday candles, sparkler (if your child wants one), and matches or lighters well in advance. Anything you can do ahead of time saves your energy for the party.

Do make sure the cake is big enough so that everyone can have a generous piece. Don't skimp and wind up with a cake that's too small.

Don't buy ice-cream cake or ice cream in exotic flavors like almond mint or pistachio marshmallow. Choose simple flavors like chocolate, vanilla, and strawberry, unless the birthday person doesn't like them.

Don't take the ice-cream cake out at the last minute, or you won't be able to cut it. When the party begins, remove the cake from the freezer and put it in the refrigerator. That way it will be thawed enough to get a knife through when the time comes to serve it—approximately forty-five to sixty-five minutes into the party. (Check the directions for proper thawing time on the cake box.)

Do make sure to have a container of tofutti or sorbet on hand as an alternative to ice cream or ice-cream cakes for any child who might have an allergy to dairy products. (Find out about this ahead of time, if possible.)

Don't plan any paper decorations for the top of the cake. Little paper umbrellas may be beautiful, but placed close to lit candles, they can go up in flames.

Do buy good-quality birthday candles. But be forewarned: Some candles may be overwaxed at the tips and might take an abnormally long time to light. For this reason, arm yourself with two new disposable lighters instead of matches.

Do place the candles on one side of the cake so the birthday person won't have to lean over to blow them out. Singed chins are no fun. On the other hand, don't clump the candles too close together or they'll be difficult to blow out and frustrating to the child.

PARTY STAPLES

TABLEWARE, FAVORS & INVITATIONS

It's time for your birthday party shopping trip. Make a list of what you want to purchase or order before you go. The list should include:

Paper goods (plates, cups, napkins, tablecloth).

Plastic goods (utensils and cups).

Decorations.

Candles and **trimmings** for the birthday cake.

Materials for games, art projects, and special items (a tarpaulin for picnicking on the ground or the floor?).

Invitations, favors, and prizes.

Your child should be allowed to accompany you on the shopping trip. If the birthday person is very young, consider doing the shopping in two parts. If for any reason he doesn't want to come along, forget it. Don't make him feel bad about it.

For most children, the shopping trip is an adventure that stimulates their fantasies about the party and their excitement about entertaining their friends.

. . . .

Table Trimmings

Here's a chance for the birthday person to express his sense of color and design. If you don't like the plates, cups, napkins, and table-cloth he chooses, keep it to yourself. Remember, it's not your party. If your child wants black plates, let him have black plates.

Noisemakers and Whistles. If you give them out, you are risking broken eardrums and may end up hollering at the kids to stop making so much noise. That's unfair. Noise also destroys order and breaks down the structure of the party, since parents may not be heard over the din. Avoid noisemakers and whistles.

Paper Goods. Look for sturdy paper plates that don't bend. If the plates the birthday person chooses are flimsy, buy doubles so that they won't bend and spill the food. For a party meal, you'll need 9- or 11-inch plates and large napkins, and a set of small plates or bowls (get bowls for two- and three-year-olds) and small napkins for the ice cream and cake. Napkins, cups, and tablecloths are usually available in the same design.

Party Hats. Don't bother buying them, either. If your child really wants to have them make sure he knows that some children won't want to wear them. If you are buying hats anyway, avoid the under-the-chin-strap types, which pinch, snap, and can even hurt. Get headbands, crowns, or hats that fit down over the head—like Mickey Mouse caps. (Remember, never give the pointed, dunce cap kind because the point is dangerous.) Make sure you have masking tape and a stapler handy to repair the hats that fall apart.

Place Cards. Don't buy them. Place cards only cause trouble and unhappy guests. "I don't want to sit *there*!" "I want to sit by Stevie!" After all, who wants to be made to sit with a nerd on one side and a cousin on the other? Children like finding their own seats—only intervene if there's a problem.

Plastic Goods. It may be a breach of etiquette, but the only eating utensil you should buy and set out for young children is the spoon. *Don't buy forks.* They're inappropriate utensils at any party for children six and under. That goes for eating cake, potato salad, or anything else. You don't need any guests at the table getting stabbed in the face.

Use your own spoons if you have enough of them, but if you're going to buy plastic spoons, choose heavy ones that will not snap off or chip when you put them in food. (The flimsy kind that break and chip into little pieces can choke a child.) If you really can't stand the idea of witnessing children eating only with spoons, then plan to let them use their fingers and buy plenty of extra napkins.

If you decide on plastic cups instead of paper cups, again, choose ones that are heavy. The flimsier the cup, the more frequent will be the spills. There are bound to be some spills, but there's no point in increasing the odds.

. . . .

Decorations

Decorating ideas will be discussed in the next chapter, but while you're shopping, stock up on some of the following supplies:

- ☆ **A large poster board (for the front-door marquee)**
- **Balloons**
- **Brightly colored Magic Markers**
- **Glitter and glue**
- **String, yarn, and ribbon**
- **Paper and plastic toys (optional)**
- **Construction paper**
- **Crepe paper**
- **Double-sided tape**
- **Colored light bulbs and Christmas lights**
- **Bulb blinker sockets**

. . . .

For Theme Parties

Themes can be a useful coordinating tool. They can set the tone, add color and fun, and make a party special. If Thanksgiving, Valentine's Day, St. Patrick's Day, the Fourth of July, or another such holiday is close to your child's birthday, you should consider using it as a theme. Spring, summer, winter, and fall also have thematic possibilities.

Some themes that may be meaningful to the birthday person are easier to coordinate than you would think. For example, if your child likes dinosaurs, rainbows, or frogs, you will have no trouble finding accessories to match, such as plates, cups, napkins, table decorations, and favors from T-shirts to stickers. (Remember, too, that if you don't see what you're looking for, a plain paper cup with a rainbow sticker becomes a rainbow cup.)

If you give a theme party, do it in the simplest way possible. Here are some possible theme parties:

Colors Parties. These are the easiest ones to do, and they're lots of fun for the children. At a yellow party, for instance, all the guests can wear yellow, and the balloons, streamers, cookies, cake frosting, and drinks can also be yellow.

Fourth of July Parties. Tell everyone to wear red, white, and blue. Decorate the table with American flags, little battleships, or space ships that reflect a patriotic theme.

Number Parties. For a "big five" birthday party for a five-year-old, for instance, put 5's on all the decorations you make. Guests can be given everything in fives—invitations cut in the shape of 5, five M&M's candies, five small cookies, five party favors. Fives can be printed on balloons and drawn on place mats.

ST. PATRICK'S DAY

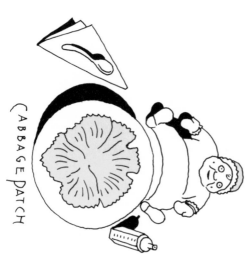

CABBAGE PATCH

Pirate Parties. Pass out bandanas and adhesive moustaches when the guests arrive. Select pirate plates, cups, tablecloth, and napkins. Have a treasure hunt as part of the entertainment.

St. Patrick's Day Parties. Ask the guests to wear green clothing or a green accessory. Pin a shamrock to each child when he comes in. Have a green cake and green decorations. Put a drop of green food coloring in the soda.

Superhero or Cartoon Character Parties. Buy the corresponding paper goods

VALENTINE'S DAY

EASTER BUNNY

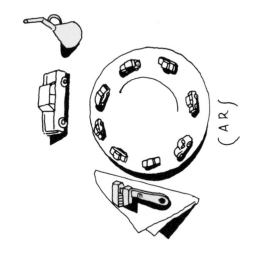

(CARS)

and use the toys to decorate the table. Try to think of a game that relates to the theme.

Valentine's Day Parties. Write instructions on the invitation for your guests to wear red, and trim the birthday room in red. Have red balloons, red candles on the cake, red flowers, and red decorations on the table.

Consider the *gender* of the theme. Don't use G.I. Joe toys or a Barbie doll as a theme for a coed party. If you're inviting seven-year-old boys to a girl's party, don't ask everyone to wear pink.

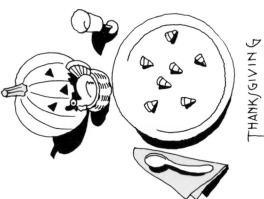

THANKSGIVING

G.I. JOE

. . . .

Party Favors and Prizes

Don't be the well-intentioned grandmother who gives underwear or socks for birthdays. I know one mother who went to a lot of trouble making beautiful knitted stocking caps as party favors. The children picked the caps up, said "Nice" in unenthusiastic voices, and put them down quickly to go play. Favors should be fun.

Some people like to give one present to each child. I believe that kids prefer more items even if they're small and inexpensive. I like to think of these objects as cultured junk. For three to four dollars per child, you can buy some small, entertaining favors to fill a plastic or paper party bag.

You have not done a good job if you've made the things in every party bag different. Make sure that the favors are all identical whenever possible. Don't buy boy favors and girl favors. What if a girl wants a Transformer toy? What if a boy wants a Care Bear animal? If you give metal cars, they should all be the same model and the same color. If they're different, someone is bound to feel cheated. A rule of thumb you can count on is that somebody else's always looks better.

I've found that if I mean to put twenty-five identical party favors in party bags, but somehow make a mistake so that two items are not the same, those two things become the objects that kids notice most. If you find that you are one yo-yo short, take out all of the other yo-yos or you're going to spoil the party for the one yo-yo-less child.

Try to buy toys the children can do something with. Doing is always the most fun. They will enjoy pretend fangs, a moustache they can stick to their upper lip, a pair of toy spectacles, a plastic nose they can use as part of a disguise, a puzzle, or small wind-up toys. Play money, rubber fingers, and glow-in-the-dark presents will also be great hits, as will sturdy Styrofoam airplanes that seven- to nine-year-olds can easily assemble. (Remember to explain beforehand that the planes are for *outdoor* use only.) If you're having a theme party, you may be able to limit the favors to related colors or objects ("Let's see how many red things we can get!")

Prizes can be similar to party favors: They'll seem different because they're not in the party bags and they're not being handed out to all the guests. Glow-in-the-dark shoelaces or balls, Matchbox cars, and paper airplanes make good prizes. If you're going to have a treasure hunt, remember to buy the treasures when you go on your party shopping trip.

DO'S AND DON'TS

When you're selecting party favors, keep these points in mind:

Don't give out favors that can be dangerous to the children or their younger siblings. Look out for sharp edges and points. Also watch out for the swallow factor. Children should not choke on their presents.

Don't give children gum or candy for party favors. Some parents don't approve, and there's no point in having gifts that will create conflict or disappointment.

Don't give out lollipops. Children can fall down with them in their mouths.

Don't give out water pistols unless it's an outdoor summer party and the children are wearing bathing suits.

Don't give out toys that require electrical batteries unless you also give the children the batteries they'll need.

. . . .

Invitations

Your child may be very picky about the invitations. They are the introduction to the party, and the birthday person will probably have definite ideas about what he wants.

Be creative. If you're planning a trip to a skating rink or the zoo, how about having invitations in the shape of an ice skate, or monkey, or elephant's head? Or, since you're treating the party as theater, why not have invitations that look like tickets to a Broadway show? To be thoroughly modern, you might try a computer printout invitation. If you and the birthday child are making the invitations yourselves, be sure to buy what you need to give them a special look, and remember to buy or make colorful envelopes that will enhance the packaging. Brightly colored stickers can be a great help here.

After your shopping trip, you can take your next step for the party by filling out the invitations.

The birthday invitation must contain all the critical information. Just like a newspaper article, it should answer all the **W**'s. **W**hat is it? **W**ho's it for? **W**hen is it? **W**here is it?

The invitation should tell:

What kind of party it is. It's a birthday party.

Who the party is for. It's for Eric Hoffstead. Use your child's first and last names. Allow no room for confusion.

Which birthday it is. It's Eric's fourth birthday. Or, he'll be four years old.

When the party will be (the day and the date). It's Thursday, February 24 (not simply February 24).

How long it will last. The party is from 4:30 P.M. to 6:00 P.M. If it's necessary for the guests to be right on time, let the parents know. Say something like "Show Begins

Promptly." Or, if you want to be more subtle, "Amy is looking forward to seeing you, so please be on time!"

Whether or not parents should stay. If you don't want adults there, write "Drop-off time. . . . Pick-up time. . . ." If you do want adults there, say so. "Parents, please stay with your child. We will have wine and cheese for you."

The meal plan. If you are not going to have a meal, say, for instance, "Come to Fred's birthday party for Magic, Cake, and Ice Cream." If you are going to have a meal, say, "This is a Birthday Lunch Party," or, "This is a Birthday Pizza Party." If you don't let parents know, you will have lunch guests who've already been fed. Since parties are the most fun when all the children participate equally, don't forget to inform them in advance.

Special instructions. If your activity is going to be an art project, for instance, put a note on the invitation asking guests to come in old clothes.

Directions. If your house or the party place is hard to find, include a small map to guide guests to the spot. Give instructions on how to get to the zoo if necessary.

Where to meet. For parties outside the home, make sure the parents know where to drop off their children. Say, "Meet us in the zoo parking lot," or, "upstairs at the Green Tulip."

RSVP. Make sure to put your address and telephone number on the card for a response. If you want to hear by a particular date, write, "Please RSVP by ____" (for example, Tuesday, May 24).

Make your invitations say exactly what you want them to say. Practice on a piece of paper before filling them in.

Here are three different, well-done party invitations:

THINK PINK!

You're invited to

PATTI PERRY'S

5th Birthday Party!

Tuesday June 18

2:30—4:00 P.M. The Perrys' House

322 Earl St., Newton

PLEASE WEAR PINK

to match the cake and
the surprises

RSVP by June 10, 555-1131

★ WE WANT YOU! ★

FOR

SAM'S 7th BIRTHDAY PARTY

You're invited on
Sunday, May 19
From 4:30 to 6:00 P.M.
For Sam Penn's Birthday Party
There'll be music &
magic & pizza &
fun & prizes!
We'll be waiting at Sam's house
410 Park St., Irvington
Please call Mrs. Penn
at 555-1116

and let us know if you'll

TAKE A HIKE WITH MIKE!

YOU'RE INVITED TO
MIKE COLEMAN'S 9TH BIRTHDAY PARTY

Thursday, July 14
Meet at *Mike's* house
410 Orchard St.
Elmsville
10:00 A.M. sharp!
Backpacks & Hikers' Lunch
will be provided
Wear sneakers & tough clothes, please

Mike's Dad will bring
you home before three o'clock

RSVP 555·1313

Finally, plan ahead. Don't hand out the invitations only a few days before your child's birthday party—too many children won't be able to come. And don't have the birthday person hand out the invitations at school. Half of them will never get home.

Mail out the invitations so that they arrive *at least* three to four weeks in advance. (When you're getting the addresses, be sure to write down the guests' phone numbers on a separate piece of paper to keep with you during the party in case of emergency.) If children or their parents haven't called to let you know whether they're coming, check with them a few days before the party. You can just say, "We were worried about whether you got the invitation to Rachel's party on Thursday, and I'm calling to make sure you did."

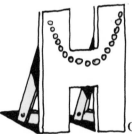ow you want to set up
the stage and props is something you should plan before
the day of the party. The first rule of thumb is to do as
many things as you can in advance (see the Party Planning
Checklist in the back of the book). Of course, if your party
is at a gym, zoo, or museum, you will only need to concern
yourself with the table or the ground tarp. If it's at home or
in a room at a restaurant, you'll have additional tasks in
readying the space.

If your child is old enough, let him help you make and put up the
decorations. The work may be slower and less efficient, but the pleasure he will have in participating is well worth the extra time.

. . . .

The Marquee

Remember Broadway, and the excitement you feel when you see the marquee on the theater announcing the name of the show and the names of the stars. For a birthday party, the more you can establish the festive atmosphere with the first things the party guests see, the more anticipation you will build and the less you'll have to prove that the party *is* exciting. From the moment the kids see the sign on the front door announcing Sandra's Birthday Party, they'll know they're in for something special.

Start with a large poster board. Write the name of the star and the event of the day on it in big, bright, thick Magic Marker letters: NICOLE'S BIRTHDAY PARTY. You can glue on a glossy black-and-white photograph of the birthday person if you want to underline the theatrical atmosphere.

If your child has special decorating ideas—paper airplanes, stickers, Cheerios cereal, or the names of the guests—encourage him.

Make the marquee several days or even a week before the party. On the day of the party, put it up and tape balloons to it, so that the children will see it coming down the block or the hallway outside your apartment.

If you're having the party at a restaurant, ask the management if you may set the marquee up at the spot where the guests will be greeted. (Take along thumbtacks and masking tape.) Then put another, smaller sign on the door of the party room so people will know exactly where to go. The marquee introduces the event and helps build the anticipation.

. . . .

The Entrance Hall

This space sets the tone for the party. It's best to set the decorations up the day before the party to give yourself time for improvements.

If you're looking for inspiration, think about how new supermarkets and gas stations decorate when they open. They string very simple

flags along ropes that are stretched across open spaces. Cut out trian-
gles from construction paper and attach their wide side every five
inches to strings that run from next to the front door to the other side of
the hallway. Make sure the decorations hang low enough so that the
children will see them as they walk in. Alternatively, string large cutouts of the number of your child's birthday (like, 4, 4, 4, 4) across the
wall or ceiling. Crepe paper or strings of Christmas lights will also work
in the hallway, as will 25- or 40-watt green, blue, yellow, and red light
bulbs in party lantern holders. (Inexpensive screw-in, bulb blinker
sockets, available at hardware stores, will create a carnival effect.)

If you are having a particular color as a theme, add anything and
everything you can think of that is in that color to the entranceway—
for instance, blue balloons, blue streamers, blue flags, and blue
light bulbs.

Another easy way to decorate the entranceway is with balloons
(check the Yellow Pages for suppliers). Make sure the balloons don't
lose air and look limp by the time guests arrive. Latex balloons last for

72

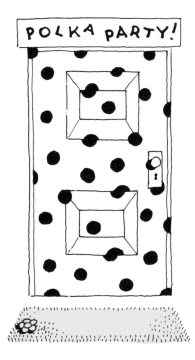

two to three hours before they start deflating; Mylar balloons—the shiny metallic kind—are more expensive, but they can last as long as seven to ten days. Always blow up fresh nonhelium balloons no more than a couple of hours before the party. If you're having helium balloons delivered, get them the day of the party, right before the party begins, if possible, so they're freshly filled. Order four or five extra ones to replace those that will inevitably get broken at the party.

Buy all the helium balloons in the same color and tie them all with the same color yarn (to avoid color wars). They'll make a colorful, cloudlike ceiling above the reach of the children, and the guests will each get to take one home when they leave. These are "guest-degradable" decorations.

When you've completed the entranceway, check your efforts. Go out the front door with the birthday person and walk in together. Is the effect dramatic? Fun? Different? Do you feel as if you're entering a festive place? If not, see what else you can add to make it more exotic. A red light bulb in the hallway socket? Some extra balloons?

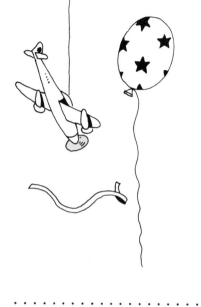

Marking Out the Territory

f you are having the party in your home, you'll want to keep all the guests together in one area where everything related to the birthday party is going to happen. You don't want children wandering off into other rooms, getting lost or distracted.

 DO'S AND DON'TS

To mark out the party space:

Do close all the doors to rooms that are off limits. Tape the cellar door shut.

Do dim the lighting in any area that is open, but not party territory. Turn the lights down as low as possible or leave only one small light on to create an uninviting look.

Do cut large, bright arrows or footprints out of cardboard and tape them to the floor to guide the guests on their way from the party room to the bathroom—this will create a party thoroughfare. You can also tape a straight or

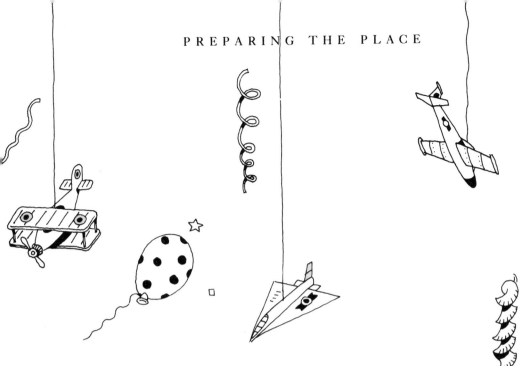

squiggly line on the floor or along the wall. Paper tape, available in neon colors at most stationery and art supply stores, is usually a safe bet; however, you should be sure not to use vinyl tape! It will take color out of the walls, floor, and carpet. Pretest a piece of any tape in an obscure place on your floor or carpet to make sure that it won't pull up the color. You don't want your house to have a permanent ghost of the party.

☆

☆ Party-Proofing Measures

Remove all the extra pieces of furniture from the area you're planning to use, and store them in another room. Beware of the consequences, though, when you move the dining room table away and leave a low-hanging chandelier, or expose outlets and wiring by taking the bed out of someone's room. Put electrical tape over the outlets—and tape the wiring to the wall. The old adage "Better safe than sorry" is nowhere more applicable than when you're turning your home over to a crowd of young people.

75

DO'S AND DON'TS

Some tips on preparing the party room:

Do put away the breakable green vase that you've always loved. Don't say, "Be careful of the green vase!" Rather than going around the party saying "No! No, no!" remove anything breakable within range of children's hands.

Do put brightly colored paper tape around the edge of all glass-topped tables.

Do take down pictures and mirrors that are hanging along the party thoroughfare. If they're loose, they're liable to be knocked down and broken.

Do put a big sign on large mirrors and sliding glass doors announcing DAVID'S PARTY, or attach colorful decals or neon tape. The reason for this, of course, is so that no one tries to walk into or through them! If these measures aren't possible, then have the party in a different room.

Do secure all three-legged pedestal tables. These are easily pulled over by children and can be quite damaging to them.

Do put away the fireplace shovel and poker. They're potential weapons.

Do put the knife rack away. Put away the choppers. If you have blades by Hoffritz, nobody wants to know about it. Tape the knife drawer shut.

Do put a gate on the stairs. Even if your child is used to the stairs and is well behaved, don't assume others are.

Do take away all little slippery rugs or tape them down. (Don't find yourself saying when it's already too late, "Oh, I should have warned you about that little rug!")

Do remove all chairs that are ready to fall apart. You do not want chairs collapsing and children getting hurt.

Don't use folding chairs if the party is for very young children. They stand on chairs, and folding ones can collapse and trap them.

Do put away your remote-control units, and cover your computer. Put away the VCR tapes that you don't want erased. Tape over control units on your VCR so they won't get jammed by little fingers.

Do ask your child, if he is five or older, which toys can be left out for his friends and which should be put away for safekeeping. If he's younger than five, put away *all* his toys. Hide them. Lock them up if necessary. The reasons for this are abundant: (1) The birthday person may not want to share his toys. (2) His toys may get broken. (3) Children fight over toys—"I didn't get my turn with his truck!"—and you don't want any fights or tears or unhappiness at this birthday party. (4) Toys can be projectiles. They break other things and can hurt children.

Do tape the bathroom lock open (for preschool guests) and have a wrench handy in case anyone gets locked in.

Do tape the light switch "on." You don't want children going into the bathroom in the dark and getting scared.

Do tape the medicine cabinet closed.

Do put paper cups by the bathroom sink in case children want to take a drink of water.

Do put away bottles and blades.

Do put out an extra box of tissues and an extra roll of toilet paper. The children may be too polite (or too embarrassed) to say something about it if you run out of toilet paper. Put the extra roll of toilet paper on the floor underneath the dispenser.

· ·

Setting Up the Party Room

N ow you're ready to arrange the party room. Don't get carried away with decorations. Five or ten minutes after they've entered, the children won't notice them. It's a waste of energy, for instance, to hang streamers from the ceiling. No one will be looking up.

The only decorations that make any sense are dual purpose, and they're for younger children. For two-year-olds, for instance, buy big, colorful, soft foam-rubber balls that the guests can play with and take home. The balls brighten up the room and serve as party favors. Instead of focusing on the trimmings, your attention should go toward creating a stage and eating area.

· · · · · · · · · · · · · · ·

Preparing the Stage

If you're having an entertainer, ask yourself: Where can he perform?

An open space that's far from the door is ideal. This is the quietest and the least distracting area, because it is separated from noise and movement that will conflict with the party. If you're in a restaurant, the children should face the stage with their backs to the door, so they won't see the waiters, diners, or parents coming and going. Chairs are not necessary—the audience can sit on the floor.

Check the backdrop that will be behind the entertainer. It should not be distracting. A blank wall is better than a picture window—it will offer no glare and no motion to compete with the performance. Also make sure there are some extra lights; two standing lamps, for instance, will brighten up the stage.

. . . .

Preparing the Eating Area
. . . .

If one part of a room in a restaurant must be close to the door and the noise and motion, use that for the eating area rather than the stage.

It is not absolutely necessary to borrow or rent tables and chairs for an at-home birthday party that you can't accommodate at your table. A water-resistant ground cover from a sporting goods store is more than adequate. Set up the dining area picnic style—in the living room, playroom, bedroom, or any appropriate area. However, if you're renting a room in a restaurant, *do* have the children dine at the table. Eating on the floor of a public restaurant is not the same as eating on the floor at home.

Leave the space between the stage and the eating area as empty as you can make it. The diagram shows the ideal setup for a room in a restaurant.

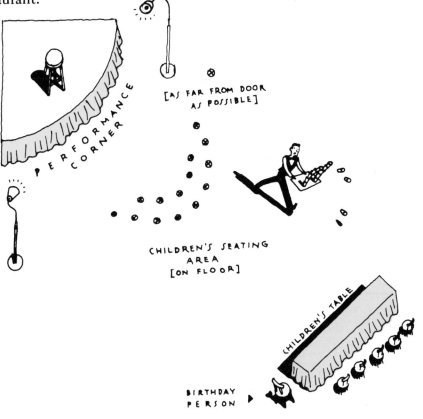

PERFORMANCE CORNER

[AS FAR FROM DOOR AS POSSIBLE]

CHILDREN'S SEATING AREA [ON FLOOR]

CHILDREN'S TABLE

BIRTHDAY PERSON ▶

79

. . . .

Setting the Table

The table at a birthday party for anyone under eight should be set in a minimalist way. It is not necessary to use your good china and silverware, your best crystal and silver candelabra. Why invite catastrophe?

Put down two or three soft old tablecloths, or a utility cloth to absorb spills, before spreading out the paper birthday party tablecloth. (There will be spills. If there are not spills, count yourself among the blessed few.) Have a standby tablecloth in the wings in case a huge spill ruins or makes holes in the paper cloth. If you have plenty of helpers and a sensitivity to mess (which your guests will not share), you may also want to use the standby tablecloth after the meal and before the cake to replace the one that's littered with food.

Lay out the napkins and plastic spoons before the party if you wish, but do not set out plates and do not have food waiting on the table when the children sit down. Keep the plates and food in the kitchen or in a separate serving area so you can make a ceremony out of distributing them after the children are seated.

. . . .

Table Decorations

. . . .

In my view, the best table decorations are "guest degradable" and can be eaten or taken home. A lineup of four little chocolate cars wrapped in red foil, a few chocolate kisses, or a small, colorful paper cup filled with nuts, raisins, and mini-marshmallows will look and taste good. Dual-purpose tableware—for instance, reusable plastic straws and cups—also look good and can be taken home by the guests. Small wind-up toys they can play with at the table are another good idea.

If you're having a theme party, there will probably be many related centerpieces available—accordion-pleated Valentines, turkeys (if the birthday is near Thanksgiving), or even Mickey Mouse figures. You can also use something you already have, such as a Cabbage Patch doll (with a handmade birthday crown on its head), a Transformer toy, or a GI Joe Hovercraft plane (with a few flowers stuck down in the galley, if you like). Your centerpiece can be as simple as a low bowl of flowers or fruit. You don't have to get fancy to make the table look colorful and festive.

DISASTERS TO AVOID

Candles should not be used on the table. They may be pretty, but burning candles can be knocked over and cause a fire.

Large vases of flowers that block the children's view of one another should not be placed in the middle of the table. Remember, seated children are lower than seated grown-ups.

Streamers or ribbons should not be stretched across the table. They can be pulled accidentally (or on purpose) by small hands.

. . . .

Music

No one wants to listen to sing-along songs during a party. Do not have "children's music" playing—even if the party is for two- or three-year-olds.

Pleasant soft rock music, the kind played by Billy Joel, The Mamas and the Papas, and the early Beatles, makes a good party background. Select your music ahead of time and have it set up and playing when the guests arrive. Put tapes or records near the machine. The guests may not consciously notice the music, but it adds to the festivities. Think supermarket.

. . . .

Lighting

Children like light. They *love* being in bright rooms and find darkness and shadows creepy. Put 60- to 75-watt bulbs instead of 40-watt bulbs in the lamps that are in party territory—as long as the shades will tolerate them. Don't simply take the shades off the lamps. That makes the light harsh and unpleasant.

Plan to leave yourself plenty of time after preparing the place to have some rest, take a shower, and change clothes for the party. It's essential that the birthday parents be relaxed and ready—in top form for the party.

PREPARING THE IMPORTANT

In the theater, we call the kind of rehearsal you need for the birthday party a gypsy run-through. The show is run through from beginning to end, with stops for adjustments.

For the birthday party, you can do a lot of the preparation by talking over the specifics with the important people. These people are: **1** the birthday person, **2** the siblings, **3** the helpers, and **4** relatives who may be joining the party.

Preparing the Birthday Person

Go over what will happen at the party from beginning to end. Rehearse the details with the birthday person:

Saying Hello. This is an opportunity to bone up on good manners. Talk to your child about how to greet people. Then pretend you're the guest and let him say hello and show you inside.

Opening the Presents. It's great to get gifts, but whether to open them at the party or after the party is something you must resolve with your child well ahead of time. Particularly for children under the age of seven, I recommend *no* opening of presents at the party. Letting a four-year-old open presents is like playing Russian Roulette with the feelings of the guests. The dangers are many, if not to the birthday person himself, then to the other children, who are bound to feel some tension, jealousy, or competitiveness.

"That's just like Jason's. Jason doesn't like his!"

"Ah, that's not such a good present. My present is better!"

"I already have that. It doesn't work very well."

Saying Thank You. Make sure your child knows how to respond when someone hands him a present, even if he won't be opening it at the party. He should always say "Thank you," and look the person he's speaking to in the eye. The birthday person should carry the present inside and put it in the place presents go. Be certain he knows where that is.

If the birthday person is opening presents at the party, have him practice looking directly at the giver of the gift saying, "Thank you," or "That's really nice!" Talk about the meaning of gifts and how important it is for him to acknowledge the time, care, and feelings involved when someone has picked out a present for him—even if he's not absolutely crazy about the gift itself. He doesn't have to gush, but a thank-you is always in order.

Rehearse with the birthday person how, at the end of the party, he should look each person in the eye and say "Thank you for coming. Thank you for the present."

The Birthday Cake. Ask your child whether he wants to blow out the candles by himself. It may be that he'd really prefer everybody to help him. Tell him that you're planning to give him the first piece of cake after he has blown out the candles. If he says he wants the last piece instead, let him identify which piece he'd like before you begin to serve, and save it for him.

The Birthday Seat. Identify which seat the birthday person would like to sit in at his party. Does he want to sit higher than the other guests? If he does, put the Yellow Pages on his chair.

Party Favors. Let the birthday person know where you will put the favors or party bags, and find out whether he would like to help hand them out.

Preparing the Siblings

Birthday parties are hard on younger and older brothers and sisters because they often feel left out. They should be given some special attention during the introductions and the cake ceremony, but they need to know that the birthday child will be getting the greatest recognition today.

It may help younger siblings to keep themselves from crying (when they don't get presents at the door and are not allowed to blow out the candles) if they know there will be a surprise waiting for them at the end of the party. It's a good idea to have a gift for siblings to open when the birthday child is opening his presents. Even the most selfless children are bound to experience some jealousy of their brother or sister's riches.

A good way to make siblings feel special and important to the success of the party is to ask their help. Don't enlist them for cleanup afterward. Good jobs for brothers and sisters include: (1) taking coats from guests and hanging them up (if the sibling is big enough), (2) passing out potato chips or cookies, and (3) showing the little children where the bathroom is.

Don't ask siblings to do something that puts them at risk of looking foolish. They need to feel competent. For instance, don't have them carry drinks. They would hate spilling anything and making a mess. Give them support. Don't take their job away by forgetting what you'd asked them to do or by changing your mind—*even if their help makes it harder for you*. If siblings feel useful at the party, they'll have fun, too.

Go over the party schedule with the birthday person's siblings; delineate their responsibilities.

Greetings and Introductions. If you'll need their help in answering the door, siblings should be prepared on how to greet the guests and introduce themselves.

Handling Feelings of Jealousy. Acknowledge that they may wish it was their special day, but it isn't. When it's their birthday party, they'll get to be the center of attention, but this is the birthday person's party.

Not Being a Stinker or Spoiler. Talk to siblings about how they should *not* behave. Stinkers and spoilers call names, ridicule, and diminish in importance something that's special to someone else. They trivialize and undermine the event by saying things like "Who cares if you got X, Y, or Z, I got . . . !" Tell them how important this party is to their sister or brother, and remind them how important their party will be to them. Invoke the Golden Rule.

Preparing the Helpers

Preparing the helpers before the party is vital. They should know that they are at the party as your assistants, not as guests or idle observers. Alertness to their duties will make all the difference between a smooth or bumpy party.

If you're having twelve or more children, you'll need at least three people to assist you with the food and activities. They can be teenagers, older siblings and relatives, friends, or other parents. If the party is outside the home, make sure that at least one of your helpers can drive, and brings along a license in case of an emergency. Have a helper park the car.

Jobs you should assign to helpers include:

- Taking off coats and boots when children arrive.

- Hanging up coats, setting out boots.

- Taking Polaroid pictures of each child.

- Running the video camera.

- Taking party pictures for the family album (don't count on this person to do anything else).

- Engaging new arrivals while the birthday person and parents answer the door and greet the other guests.

- Taking young children to the bathroom.

- Helping out with games and projects, particularly with young children.

- Changing the music tapes or records (a two-hour cassette is far superior to an LP that must be flipped every twenty to thirty minutes).

- Refilling cups or plates at the table.

- Mopping up spills (let them know where the paper towels will be in the main room).

- Turning off the music when it's time for the cake ceremony and putting it back on again afterward.

- Holding the extra disposable lighter.

- Lowering and raising the lights during the birthday cake ceremony.

- Holding the door open for the cake presentation.

- Putting the video cassette into the VCR and turning it on when the children are ready to watch "the show."

- Helping children on with their coats and boots at the end of the party.

Go over the party schedule with your helpers. Let them know that some of the time they won't be doing very much, but they must be standing by for pivotal moments and unexpected mishaps. If a child splits his pants and needs to be changed, let the helpers know where you have set out new clothing for just such an emergency.

. . . .

Preparing the Grandparents, Aunts, and Uncles

liminate difficulties from the relatives by talking with them ahead of time. Well-meaning grandparents may feel that they need to pay monumentally special attention to the birthday child at the party. Give them dispensation to leave the child alone. Tell them they should be observers, not participants. Tell them who is answering the door and let them know if you're not going to be opening presents. They may want Jimmy to open their presents before the party, if they will not be able to stay around afterward.

If Uncle Jake smokes cigars, ask him not to do so before or during the party. The same goes for Aunt Betty and cigarettes.

. . . .

Preparing the Family Animals

hat should you do about the family dog? Is there any way to prepare him? Even if you have a totally relaxed, angelic animal who lies quietly in the corner and lets children climb on his back, some guests will be frightened of him. The best solution is to spare your dog the party and vice versa! Let him relax at a friend's house or in another room.

The same formula goes for all your other pets. Be kind to animals; keep them away from the guests.

rom the opening curtain to the last goodbye, how do you run the show? How do you establish the mood, maintain the pace, and enhance the spirit of the party?

Put on your director's hat. You're the person who'll be sitting in the director's chair with stopwatch in hand. You're in charge of the timing. The actors will play their parts, but they need you for cues, directions, and transitions. You're the one telling them what this show is all about and making sure the performance is the best it can be.

Because the schedule is so important, it helps if you write out an agenda and keep it on hand for reference. A small "cheat card" in your pocket will help you when you need it.

Greeting the Guests

he fun begins the moment the first guest arrives. If the party is at home, the birthday person and you can answer the door together ("There's the bell. Let's go see which one of your friends it is!"). If the party is at a restaurant or another outside-the-home place, an adult, or an adult and the birthday child, should wait by the entrance to greet the guests (you may be busy overseeing the children in a new place). Don't let a little child stand there alone. Even if it's safe, and even if he is responsible enough, a child alone doesn't *look* responsible enough.

Make the children feel welcome. Invite them in and tell them what's going to happen. Build their anticipation by letting them know the coming attractions. If the birthday person wants to announce the agenda, let him—just make sure he's rehearsed his lines. For instance:

- "Hi! Come on in! We're having a really fun party!"

- "We're going to play some games, and there are lots of prizes . . ."

- "We're going to have a magic show!"

- "We're having a big birthday cake with a sparkler on it!"

- "Wait until you see the party bags! You'll get to take one home when you leave."

. . . .

Taking Control

Establishing who's in charge is easy. When you welcome the guests, when you tell them what's happening, you're the voice of authority. Don't be timid about it. Make sure all the children can hear you, and simply announce the first activity ("Now let's begin the party with . . . a game of _____, or a really exciting project.")

If the birthday person is eight or older and wants to be in charge, your role is as a backup and support system. Intervene only if necessary. For instance, you may have to tell an excited guest that running is not allowed. You temporarily take charge by stating a party rule.

Let the children know by your demeanor and enthusiasm that this is a celebration that calls for their best behavior. Providing a summary of upcoming events at the beginning of the party will give kids a framework in which to operate. Tell them if there are any special party rules.

My first rule is always "No *gimme*'s." I say, "We're going to give away a lot of prizes today and you will all get one! But when I give a prize to someone, I don't want to hear any *gimme*'s from other people. If anyone says *gimme* to me, I'll say 'Tough Tunafish to you!'—you'll have to wait your turn."

The way to maintain control is to tell the children what is allowed and what is not allowed. Tell them directly and simply, and they'll respond. The older they are, the less you'll have to organize and control. All you'll have to do is make sure the play structure they establish does not collapse due to conflicts or unexpected events.

. . . .

What to Do with a Disruptive or Timid Child

Many children who are normally aggressive or rowdy will behave well in a new place if it's clearly special and exciting and is decorated in a festive way. This good behavior will last at least the first half hour of the party, but may extend straight through.

If a child becomes rude or obstreperous, call him on it immediately. Don't let the situation get out of hand. When a guest hits, shoves, boos, or hisses, stop the show and set things straight. Do it in front of everybody. Say,

"That's not the way we behave here. At a birthday party we are all polite to one another." Or, "You may like to have hurt feelings at your birthday party, but at this party we don't want to make anybody feel bad. We don't holler, yell, or hit."

If you have the unusual situation of a child continuing to hit or be totally uncooperative, have one of your helpers *take him out of the room*. Tell him, "We want you at the party, and you can come back when you're ready to have fun with the rest of us. But it's really not fair to the birthday person to behave the way you've been behaving."

If a child is timid or frightened, don't try to talk him out of it by assuring him that there's no reason to be afraid. Tell him he can watch the party until he decides he's ready to join in—after the first game if he wants to, or when it's time for cake and ice cream. Have one of the helpers sit with him if necessary, but don't distract yourself from the other children or keep going over to him. If he wants to join in, he probably will sooner rather than later.

. . . .

Dealing with Parents

If parents who are staying want to smoke, ask them to go outside or wait until the end of the party. Children should not have to inhale smoke during a party. It's bad for everyone, but children who are asthmatic or allergic to smoke can be thrown into an attack. You do not want to interrupt the birthday party for a trip to the hospital.

If parents disturb the party by talking, you'll have to find a way to tell them nicely to quiet down. But don't hold off just because they're grown-ups. A disruption is a disruption regardless of the source.

Maintaining the Right Pace

he first fifteen or twenty-five minutes of the party are usually a very low-key time. Let the guests look around and become familiar with the surroundings and the other children. They will move at their own pace into the spirit of the festivities. The birthday person can show his friends the birthday table, his new baby sister, the TV, or whatever is exciting in his house or at the party place.

It's always easier for latecomers to join an informal group than to join an organized activity when the party is in progress. Once most of the guests are present, use your good judgment about when to start the first activity. If the children are having a great time talking or playing with toys, let them. Don't move on to the next event unless they're ready. They can do two to five minutes more of this and less of the next activity if it's working. As captain of this ship, don't rock the boat.

Your main job in keeping the pace of the party going is to move the children smoothly from one activity into the next. Watch for good transition points. Tell them what's coming. For instance, say, "We're going to have a magic show, but first, how many people would like to play a game for prizes?" Or, "That was a great game of Bingo. Now let's start something new."

How quickly the party moves should be determined by the age of the children. With three-year-olds, for instance, you'll need to maintain a fast pace to occupy their short attention span. You may direct the children into one or two projects, such as building with blocks or making place mats, and then you may want to ask, "Who would like a picture of himself?" and take the children for pictures one by one.

Featuring the Main Event

hen it's time for the Main Event, usher the children into the theater space and have them sit down. Introduce the entertainer with enthusiasm. Do it with ceremony.

The entertainer should give all the credits for the show. He should say, "Welcome to Melissa's house! Wecome to Melissa's birthday party! Let's clap for the birthday person! Let's clap for the birthday person's sister and brother! Let's clap for the birthday person's Mom and Dad who made this party possible!" Applause adds to the theatrical spirit of the party. It makes everyone feel good, and gives the guests a chance to express their appreciation.

During the entertainer's act, he or she is in charge, and your responsibilities are on hold—unless somebody needs you. You have done what's necessary to build up to the performance; sit back and be entertained. When the event is over, applaud the entertainer. Say, "Let's clap for . . . " and begin applauding. The children will join right in.

Sitting at the Table

ow it's time for the food! And you are at the helm, again. Tell the children they should find a place at the table and get ready for the party meal and/or cake.

Of all the physical configurations at a birthday party, eating at the table is the best. It's the most cohesive group activity. It brings everyone together around a pleasurable focus.

Reserve the Birthday Person's Seat

That's the only place you need to protect. If someone else sits in it, say, "Oops! Not here! This is the birthday person's place!" Remember, let the children sit wherever else they want, but don't allow any pushing or shoving. Direct them only when it's needed.

· · · · · · · · · · · · · · ·

Serving the Food

Presenting the food is an important part of the whole event. Particularly with younger children, do as much as you can to make a ceremony out of passing each item. Start with the plates. "Here's a plate for you! And here's a plate for you!" (Remember Aunt Rivie and the way she served cottage cheese: "Here's your cottage cheese with the blueberry on top! And here's *your* cottage cheese with the blueberry on top!") Getting your food is *special*. Each child anticipates being the next in line, and is always rewarded for waiting.

The way you serve the food is the backbone of this party segment for two-year-olds. Hold their attention while they wait for their plate, their juice, their sandwich. When they're involved in the receiving game, it will be pretty easy to keep them at the table.

With three-, four-, and five-year-olds, you also can stretch out the serving into entertainment. Their anticipation for ice cream, juice, or whatever absolutely delights them. When you offer each child potato chips, say, "We have potato chips. Do you want potato chips? Yes? Here."

Tell the children the menu as you go. "We have peanut butter and jelly sandwiches and they're cut into bear shapes and duck shapes. Who wants a bear? Who wants a duck?" (Remember, there are only two choices.)

In addition to the food, you can give each child one of the party favors at the table. This will not spoil the pleasure of getting party bags at the finale, and will whet appetites for the goodies yet to come.

Always give the first present to the birthday child. Then take the second identical item out and hand it to the next child. Announce what you're doing. Share every step. "We have another surprise!" "Here's your little wind-up dog!" (And for very young children: "You hold onto him while I give the other guests their wind-up dogs! I'll be back to help you start him up!") If the favor requires a battery, show the children one that works with the battery in it, then tell them, "I'll give each of you one red dog and then I'll bring around the batteries and help you put the batteries in the dog!"

Don't bother with all this ceremony for eight-year-olds and up, however. If you do, they'll think you're a jerk. They're much more interested in the action among themselves. You should still serve the pizza, sandwiches, or whatever one by one, but it doesn't need to be so ceremonial—and you don't need to announce what you're doing item by item.

No matter what age the children are, nobody gets excused from the table to go play until *everyone* is finished eating. If a child asks, "Can I go play until it's time for cake?" the answer is "No." The idea is to have fun around the table as a group. This cohesion will build toward the cake ceremony.

· ·

The Cake Ceremony

his is the "pineapple" of the whole production, so give it the attention and drama it deserves. Make a theatrical event out of bringing in the birthday cake.

Have two light sources available, and make a big ceremony out of lowering and turning them off. Also turn off the recorded music. Light the candles and carry the cake in from a darkened area to the even darker area where the children are sitting. That's drama. That's magic. Don't bring in the cake and light the candles at the table, unless the party is for two-year-olds—and then you should never dim the lights. With three-year-olds, you can dim the lights for the cake, but watch the children's faces as you do. You don't want anyone to be frightened. If a child begins to look anxious, turn the lights back up and leave them that way.

Older children, age six and up, will like the added excitement of a sparkler burning on the cake as it's carried in; for younger children, it's more scary than exciting. This is really dramatic, but it's also dangerous because sparks do fly. If you want to use a sparkler along with the

candles, remember that even a minute or two after the sparkler has finished sparking, it's still white hot and can burn. Don't let the birthday person get burned, and don't burn yourself. (Warn him about the sparkler ahead of time so he'll know not to touch it.)

For this event, the mother plays the role of the woman in spangles at the magic show—she highlights every moment of the act. Make sure to carry an extra lighter with you in case the candles blow out on the way and threaten to spoil the moment. As you are carrying in the cake, the singing should begin. One of the helpers can start off the birthday song, and you should join in. After you place the cake in front of the birthday person, call for quiet. "Quiet, please! This is Linda's special moment! Now, make a good wish, Linda. Take your time! Good Luck!"

Blowing Out the Candles

Maintain the hushed quiet while the birthday person is wishing. When the birthday person has made her wish and begins to blow out the candles, encourage her! Don't say, "Ooh, ooh, you missed!" if she misses one flame. Cheer her on. Say, "Keep going, you can do it!" If your child doesn't want to blow out the candles, don't force her to do so. Maybe she had a bad experience once. Maybe she is suddenly afraid. A sibling, you, or the whole group can help blow out the candles if she likes.

Remember, too, that there's nothing wrong with stopping the show and starting over again if it can remedy an otherwise unhappy situation. One time when a birthday child got upset because her big sister blew out the candles, we stopped the show, relit the candles, and sang "Happy Birthday" all over again. This time the birthday child blew out her own candles and felt good.

When the birthday person finishes blowing out all the candles, applaud. She's just completed a fine performance! She's ready for praise! Give it to her!

. . . .

Passing Out Pieces of Cake

If there is one special decoration on the cake, that decoration goes to the birthday person. Say it out loud: "The birthday person gets the special decoration!"

Unless you've planned otherwise ahead of time, the birthday person always gets the first piece of cake. The second piece of cake goes to the sister or the brother. When you give out the cake, say, "The first piece goes to the birthday girl! The second piece goes to the birthday girl's brother!" By announcing what you're doing out loud, you make it clear for everyone and you remind them who's the star of today's show.

If one of your helpers makes a mistake and starts to give the birthday person's piece of cake away to someone else, stop her! Don't be reticent about it. Say, "Oops, sorry! That's the birthday person's piece of cake!"

DISASTERS TO AVOID

Trick candles (I repeat) are *not* funny! Never use them on a child's birthday cake. It is not fun to fail when you are trying to make a wish.

Jokes about the cake or the wishing are *not* funny!

Dropping the cake on the way in is *not* funny! Ice-cream cakes are hard and slippery; they can slide off the plate easily. If you drop the cake, you can ruin the moment. The event will lose some of its luster and, even if you remove the squished parts, the children may be reluctant to eat a cake that's been on the "yucky" floor.

Singed hair is *not* funny! If your daughter has long hair, make sure it's held back when she's blowing out the candles.

. . . .

Watching the Video

If you've used a video camera at the party, announce, "After the birthday cake and before we give out the party favors, we can see ourselves on TV!" Five to ten minutes of tape will interest most of the guests. Don't worry if someone walks away from the TV. Your helpers should be alert to small wanderers and keep them quietly entertained.

Narrating the film will help to hold the attention of younger children. "See, there's Alice coming in the door! There's Helen blowing out the candles!"

. . . .

Giving Out Party Bags

Hand out party bags or favors shortly before the guests leave. If you have extra time because the schedule has gone more quickly than planned, or if you want to stretch out the event, you can say, "Before I give out these bags, I want to see what's in them, I want to show you a couple of the prizes you'll be getting."

Have the birthday person give a bag to each of his guests and siblings. These are gifts from him to his friends. He can choose the order, but he should pass them out one by one. (Don't forget, of course, that the birthday person gets one, too!) Never let the children grab for their favors or party bags all at once.

If the birthday person doesn't want to distribute the favors, you can easily do it for him. One good way to fill time and build anticipation is to give the bags out in alphabetical order. "First, we'll give a bag to all the children whose name begins with K. Then, all whose name begins with L. Then M . . ." Make sure you cover all of the guests.

Saying Good-bye

Make sure that the birthday person says good-bye to each guest as he goes, and that each guest has a party bag or favor to take home. Let helpers assist the children with their coats and boots if it's cold or wet outside, so that you're free to oversee the departures and speak with the children and their parents.

When you're giving out balloons as presents, tie one on each guest's arm as he leaves so it won't blow away or go into orbit as soon as he steps outside.

After the Party

If a child is left at the party after the other guests have departed, assure him that his mother or father is on the way. If the parent is really late, you can invite the child to join the birthday person and his family while he opens his gifts.

Make a list of what present came from each guest as your child opens his gifts. Use the list for the thank-you cards.

The habit of writing thank-you notes is a good one to develop at a young age. Have the birthday person pick out the cards, or make them, before the party. If he's old enough to help but too young to write them himself, dictate and sign them within a day or two afterward, while the gifts are still fresh in his mind. It will put a good stamp on this year's birthday party.

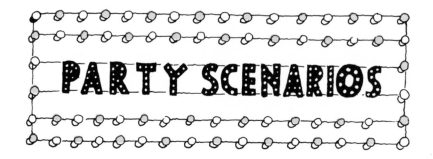

Party for Two-Year-Old Annie

DATE: Saturday, February 8

TIME: 12:00 noon to 1:00 P.M.

SETTING: The Baxter living room

CAST OF CHARACTERS: Annie, Mr. and Mrs. Baxter, Annie's four-year-old brother, two teenage helpers, Grandma Baxter, and four guests and their parents.

11:45 A.M.—One end of Baxter living room has been cleared of furniture. Padding protects corners of glass table.

Hall closet has supply of child-size and regular hangers.

Balloons printed with "Happy Birthday" line entranceway ceiling.

Mrs. Baxter removes ice-cream cake from freezer and puts it in refrigerator.

Mr. Baxter turns on soundtrack from *Annie.*

12:00 noon—First toddlers arrive with mothers and fathers.

Mother and helpers hang up coats and place gifts in corner of foyer, then Annie helps lead children into party area.

Father takes pictures on video camera as each child enters.

Grandmother offers danish pastries and coffee to moms and dads, who are seated nearby.

12:15 P.M.—Three guests are present.

Children play with foam-rubber balls, large Legos, and pliable toys on a living room carpet. Mother and helpers assist them.

12:25 P.M.—Parents accompany children to dining room and seat them. Helpers tie paper bibs around children's necks. Mr. and Mrs. Baxter pass out plates, cow- and duck-shaped sandwiches, potato chips, carrot sticks, and juice.

Helpers stand near table to assist children.

12:45 P.M.—Helper turns off party music.

Birthday cake ceremony: Mother carries in cake with three unlit candles and lights them at the table. Annie's brother helps her blow out candles, Mother cuts cake, and Grandma and helpers pass it out.

1:00 P.M.—Helpers give coats to moms and dads, who dress children to leave.

The Baxters assist Annie in giving out party bags and balloons, and saying good-bye.

Easter Bunny Theme Party
for Three-Year-Old Max

. . . .

DATE:	Saturday, March 29
TIME:	1:45 P.M. to 3:00 P.M.
SETTING:	The Embers's basement playroom
CAST OF CHARACTERS:	Max, Mr. and Mrs. Embers, Max's two older brothers, three helpers, ten guests, and their parents.

1:30 P.M.—Helium-filled balloons float along the entrance hall ceiling.

A tarpaulin is laid on the floor in one corner of playroom with bunny rabbit and Easter Egg centerpiece and napkins at each place.

Soft rock music is playing.

1:40 P.M.—First guests arrive; helpers put jackets and gifts in Max's room and escort children and moms and dads to playroom.

Mrs. Embers takes instant funny-face pictures of each guest.

Moms and dads help themselves to cheese and crackers, soda and wine, laid out near seating area.

2:00 P.M.—Helpers lead children to long, low table furnished with water-soluble markers and squares of construction paper. They help children decorate egg-shaped place mats for birthday picnic, and put each child's name on mat.

2:15 P.M.—Blocks are stacked near the art table. Children tired of decorating place mats can build a castle. Max's big brothers oversee project.

2:25 P.M.—Children are called to sit down in far corner of playroom, which has been set up for hand puppet show.

2:45 P.M.—Children are escorted back to picnic area, where they choose seats. Helpers put place mats down in front of them.

Max's brothers pass out plates and cups.

Birthday cake ceremony: Mom, Dad, and helpers serve cake (with bunny ears and whiskers), ice cream, and juice.

3:00 P.M.—Helpers collect jackets from Max's room; moms and dads dress children.

Max hands guests balloons and party bags and says good-bye.

Zoe's Fourth Birthday Party

DATE: Sunday, October 12

TIME: 2:00 P.M. to 3:30 P.M.

SETTING: Rudy's Gymnasium

CAST OF CHARACTERS: Zoe, her parents, her two older sisters, three gym teachers, and Zoe's entire class of sixteen children.

1:45 P.M.—A big sign on entrance is decorated with balloons, a picture of Zoe, and names of guests. It says HAPPY BIRTHDAY, ZOE.

2:00 P.M.—First party guests arrive wearing gym clothes, as requested on invitation. Zoe says hello and thank you for presents; stacks gifts in far corner of reception area.

Gym teachers lead children to changing room, where they take off shoes and socks and place them under bench, then escort them to gym.

2:15 P.M.—One-hour party program begins: warm-up exercises, Happy Birthday song, and 35-minute gym class. Parents watch children through one-way mirror from reception area and help themselves to cheese, fruit, wine, and soda.

3:15 P.M.—Children are brought into reception area, and sit down at tablecloth laid out on floor.

Birthday cake ceremony: older sisters help pass out cake, gym teachers serve children juice.

3:30 P.M.—Zoe and parents hand out party favors. Good-byes.

Red Fives for Johnny

DATE: Saturday, October 11

TIME: 11:00 A.M. to 12:30 P.M.

SETTING: The Mahoney kitchen (a big country kitchen)

CAST OF CHARACTERS: Johnny, Mr. and Mrs. Mahoney, Grandma Mahoney, one teenage helper, and twelve children.

10:45 A.M.—Big 5s cut out of red construction paper are strung from above door to opposite wall of kitchen. Red carnations sit in low red vase on large kitchen table.

Pizza has just been ordered.

Soft rock music is playing on cassette machine.

11:03 A.M.—First guest is dropped off at kitchen door by his mom, as requested; he is wearing red shirt.

Johnny and Mrs. Mahoney welcome him. Johnny puts present in corner.

11:15 A.M.—All guests are present. They talk and play informally in family area of kitchen.

Pizza is delivered; Grandma places box on kitchen counter and covers it with towels.

11:15 A.M.—Helper seats children on floor in circle; they play Duck, Duck, Goose.

111

11:30 A.M.—Mother gives each child a white cotton T-shirt (size 8), which has been dyed red and slipped over heavy cardboard.

Grandpa and Dad have covered kitchen table and adjacent card table (to accommodate group) with brown butcher paper, and laid out fabric markers. Children draw designs on shirts. Mrs. Mahoney tags each shirt with name of child who decorated it and puts it on a hanger to set.

11:45 A.M.—Helper gives children homemade movie tickets and shows them into den, which has been cleared of furniture.

Mr. and Mrs. Mahoney pass out paper cups filled with popcorn to children sitting in rows on floor.

11:50 A.M.—Lights are dimmed and show begins. It's a rented video tape—*The Red Balloon*.

12:10 P.M.—Children are called back to kitchen, where Grandma and helper have cleared tables and laid out red napkins at each place.

Mrs. Mahoney and helper hand out plates, then serve slices of pizza (one-half of regular slice to each child) and choice of apple juice or water.

12:20 P.M.—Birthday cake ceremony.

12:30 P.M.—Johnny and Mrs. Mahoney hand out T-shirts as parents arrive for pick up.

Pirate Pete's Sixth Birthday Party

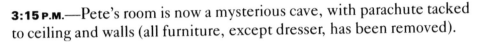

DATE: Sunday, December 7, 1986

TIME: 3:30 P.M. to 5:00 P.M.

SETTING: Pete's bedroom

CAST OF CHARACTERS: Pete, his parents, two big brothers, and twelve male friends.

3:15 P.M.—Pete's room is now a mysterious cave, with parachute tacked to ceiling and walls (all furniture, except dresser, has been removed).

3:32 P.M.—First guests arrive in pirate dress (jeans and shirts, bandanas, eye patches) and a pretend moustache that came with invitation.

Pete's father takes video footage of Pete greeting friends.

Big brothers lead guests to bedroom.

3:45 P.M.—Hunt for pirate's booty begins. Pete's brothers have hidden gold plastic coins in Pete's room and living room.

4:00 P.M.—Magician arrives and sets up in living room.

4:05 P.M.—Children trade in coins they've found for prizes.

Big brothers call them to living room, where they sit on floor for show. Magician performs tricks and teaches one to boys.

4:35 P.M.—Parents lay out tarp on floor of "pirate's cave" and serve dinner from McDonald's (burgers, fries, orange drinks).

4:50 P.M.—Birthday cake ceremony (ice-cream cake with pirate-ship decorations).

5:00 P.M.—Good-byes. Pete hands each "pirate" a bag of gold coins, raisins and nuts, and props for a magic trick.

Zoo Party for Sandi's Seventh Birthday

. . . .

DATE: Sunday, April 13

TIME: 11:00 A.M. to 1:00 P.M.

SETTING: The local zoo

CAST OF CHARACTERS: Sandi, her mom and her new husband, her dad and girlfriend, her big sister Sara, and fifteen guests.

10:50 A.M.—Sandi and her extended family wait at side of zoo entrance in parking lot. Adult helper stays home by phone.

A bunch of balloons is tied to fence with sign announcing SANDI'S BIRTHDAY PARTY.

10:55 A.M.—First guests are dropped off by parents. They talk and play quietly until all children are assembled.

11:10 A.M.—Sandi and Sara pass out name tags with each guest's telephone number and help pin them on.

11:20 A.M.—Visits to elephants, giraffes, lions, and seals during feeding time. Zoo staff member accompanies party group and tells them about care and feeding of animals.

12:00 noon—Stop at refreshment stand for lunch prearranged by parents (hot dogs, potato chips, soft drinks). Sandi's family helps serve.

Birthday cake ceremony.

12:30 P.M.—Visit to reptile house as group heads back to parking lot.

1:00 P.M.—Sandi hands out party bags and says good-bye to friends at party meeting spot, where parents wait.

Movie Party for
Alice's Eighth Birthday

. . . .

DATE: Saturday, May 17

TIME: 1:00 P.M. to 3:40 P.M.

SETTING: Jim's Soda Shoppe and the Golden Screen Cinema

CAST OF CHARACTERS: Alice, her mother and Aunt Helen, and seven guests.

12:45 P.M.—The rear booths at Jim's have been reserved for the party group.

1:00 P.M.—Girls start arriving and are seated.

1:12 P.M.—Party group is served prearranged meal of hamburgers, french fries, coke, birthday cake, and ice cream.

1:40 P.M.—Rented minibus and driver arrive at Jim's to take girls to movie theater.

1:50 P.M.—Arrive at theater (Aunt Helen has gone ahead to purchase tickets). Group goes in and takes seats.

1:56 P.M.—Aunt Helen and Mother distribute popcorn and soft drinks to anyone who wants them.

3:40 P.M.—Movie is over. Girls are each given party favor and go home with parents who wait outside theater.

Nine-Year-Old Robert's Backpacking Party

. . . .

DATE: Saturday, March 15

TIME: 11:00 A.M. to 3:00 P.M.

SETTING: The state park

CAST OF CHARACTERS: Robert, his dad, and five boy guests

10:45 A.M.—Robert and his dad are packing sandwiches into seven backpacks. Robert's dad checks his list: he has gas in car, HAPPY BIRTHDAY ROBERT sign on front door of apartment, and has packed two blankets, extra bag of potato chips, and birthday cupcakes, candles, plastic spoons, plates, and napkins in back of station wagon.

10:55 A.M.—Three friends arrive, wearing jeans, sweatshirts, and lightweight jackets.

They talk and play in Robert's room while waiting for others.

11:10 A.M.—All five guests are present.

Robert gives each guest a backpack with the guest's name stenciled on it. A bag lunch of sandwiches, potato chips, an apple, and a carton of juice is packed inside.

11:21 A.M.—Boys go downstairs and get into station wagon.

Rock music chosen by Robert plays on the tape deck, as Robert's father drives to state park.

11:55 A.M.—Group arrives at park and begins hike up medium-steep trail. Robert's father helps boys identify trees, bushes, shrubs.

12:32 P.M.—Group reaches clearing prechosen for party. Boys take off backpacks and play Freeze Tag.

Robert's father spreads picnic blankets.

12:40 P.M.—Boys sit down on blankets, take lunches from their backpacks, and eat. Birthday cupcakes are served.

1:00 P.M.—Dad distributes snap-together toy gliders for boys to fly.

1:25 P.M.—Slow hike back to car.

2:00 P.M.—Group arrives at station wagon and climbs in.

Dad heads home, stopping en route at a fast-food restaurant for drinks and bathroom.

2:04 P.M.—Car heads back to city.

Boys and dad play Sports Trivia on the way.

2:45 P.M.—Back at the apartment building. Good-byes and thank-yous. Guests take home backpacks as party favors.

PARTY-PLANNING CHECK

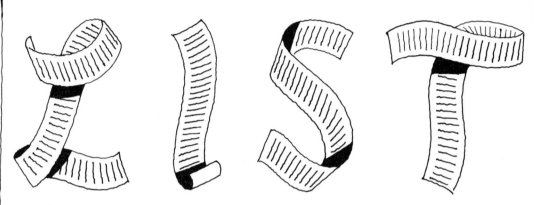

LIST

Here are some points that need to be covered when you are planning the party.

· ·

Six weeks or more before the party:

1. Who will be invited to the party?
   What ages and sexes?
   Are they classmates or a mix of friends?
2. What day of the week and date will the party be?
3. What time will it be? How long will it last?
4. Are you going to serve a meal?
5. Where will the party take place?
   If it's at home, which room?
   If outside the home, which restaurant or where will you have the meal or ice cream and cake?
6. Are you going to have a theme?
7. What will happen at the party?
   Opening activities.
   Projects and games.
   Main event.
   Party food and cake ceremony.

8. How will you decorate?
9. What kind of cake are you going to make or buy?
10. What music will be played at the party?
11. What prizes, if any, will you offer?
12. What party favors will you give out?
13. Which relatives, if any, do you want to include?
14. How many helpers will you need? Who are they?
15. What special problems indigenous to the group can you foresee and avoid?

. . . .

The week of the party:

1. Have you called the parents who haven't RSVP'd so you know who's coming?
2. Have you confirmed reservations if your party's outside the home?
3. Have you confirmed any orders or pickup times for rentals or deliveries?
4. Have you played the music you plan to use at the party?
5. Have you bought the nonperishable food for the party?
6. Have you ordered helium balloons?
7. Have you ordered the cake?
8. Have you made the marquee for the front door?
9. Do you have everything you need for putting up the decorations, including tacks, masking tape, or string?

. . . .

The day before the party:

1. Do you have enough hangers and space for coats?
2. Has the birthday cake been baked or bought?
3. Do you have the candles? Don't forget one for good luck—and *two* lighters.
4. Have you set aside an extra set of children's clothes in case of tears or spills?
5. Have you rehearsed the details of the party with:
   The birthday person? Siblings? Helpers? Grandparents, aunts, or uncles?

6. Have you reconfirmed your reservations if you're having the party at an outside place?
7. Have you confirmed the date and time of the party with the entertainer you hired?

. . . .

The night before the party:

1. Have you put a marquee on the front door?
2. Have you put lights and/or decorations up in the entranceway?
3. Have you practiced greeting procedures and thank-yous with the birthday person?
4. Have you designated the place for presents?
5. Have you moved out furniture and arranged the party space?
6. Have you put film in the camera? And *new* batteries?
7. Have you asked your child if he thinks anything was overlooked?

. . . .

The day of the party:

1. Have you added balloons to the marquee?
2. Have helium-filled balloons been delivered?
3. Are the candles and lighters in place?
4. Have you put away your child's special toys?
5. Is everything breakable removed from the party area?
6. Is there extra toilet paper in the bathroom?
7. Is the light switch taped "on" in the bathroom?
8. Is the stage set for the performance? (Don't forget the lighting.)
9. If you're serving an ice-cream cake, have you taken it out of the freezer and put it into the refrigerator before the party begins?
10. Have you set up the music?
11. Have you taken your house pet out of the party area?
12. Have you given your child a Happy Birthday Hug?

If you can answer all these questions in the affirmative, your Happy Birthday party is about to begin! Have fun!

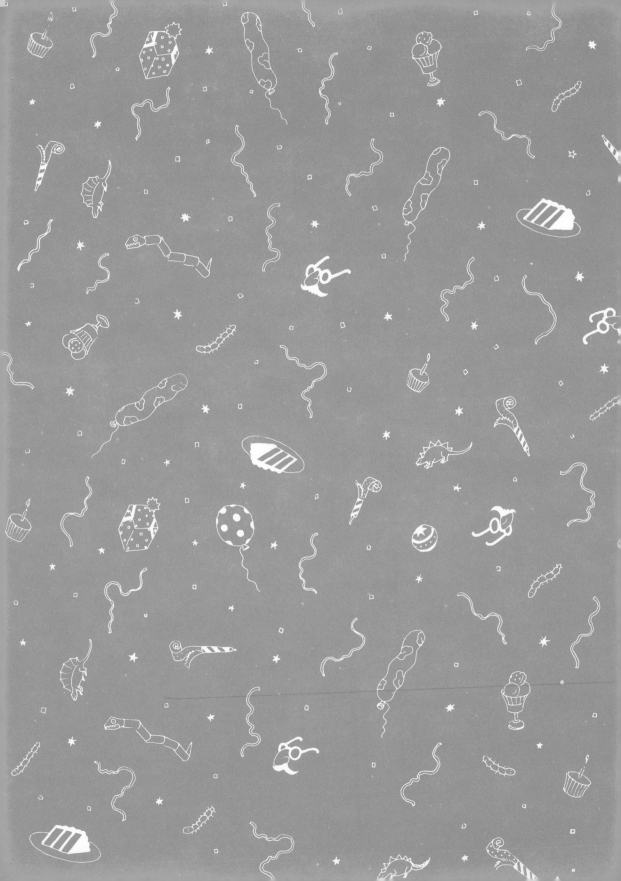